FLOWERS FOR ARRANGEMENT

SHEILA MACQUEEN

FLOWERS
for Arrangement

W. H. & L. COLLINGRIDGE LIMITED LONDON

TO THE MEMORY OF MAC

Published in 1962 by
W. H. & L. Collingridge Limited
2-10 Tavistock Street, London, W.C.2
Printed in England by
Henry Stone & Son (Printers) Ltd., Banbury, Oxon.
Second edition 1965

Contents

Vases and Containers ... ... *page* 9

Camellias Arranged with their Own Foliage ... 10

Grey Tassels and Grey-Green Leaves 12

A Mixture of Spring Bulbs 14

An Arrangement for February 16

Very Early Flowering Shrubs 18

Dried Material and Brilliant Lime Green Flowers 20

The Joy of Winter Flowers 22

Daffodils and Bright Green Moss 24

Anticipating Spring 26

A Modern Epergne 28

A Medley of Spring Flowers 30

Contrasting Tulip Shapes 32

Flowers of Late Spring 34

A Mid-Summer Arrangement 36

Peonies and Lime Flowers 38

Soft Pinks and Yellows in May 40

A 17th Century Flower Picture 42

Two Simple Rose Arrangements 44

Favourite Old-Fashioned Roses 46

Party Flowers 48

Barberton Daisies in a Beautiful Shell 52

Where Autumn Blends with Winter 54

A Basket of Summer Flowers 56

The Red Ink Plant 58

Cow Parsley from the Hedgerows 60

An Arrangement from the Water Garden ... 62

Gay Decorations for Marquees 64

Shasta Daisies 66

Grey and Silver Foliage 68

Richly-Coloured Dahlias 70

A November Group 72

A Basket of Chrysanthemums 74

Dried Flowers and Seed Heads 76

A Tropical Arrangement 78

An Indoor Garden 80

CONTENTS—*continued*

Dried Leaves and Seed Heads ...　...　*page* 82

Flowers with Short Stems　...　...　...　84

Lichen Twigs and Auratum Lilies　...　...　86

Contrasts in Texture ...　...　...　...　88

Carnations Have Prestige Value　...　...　90

Carnations and Eucalyptus　...　...　...　92

A Touch of the Orient　...　...　...　94

White Poinsettias and Foliage ...　...　...　96

An Outside Posy　...　...　...　...　98

Christmas Decorations　...　...　...　100

Preface

Flowers have had an overwhelming influence in my life ever since a chance encounter with the late Constance Spry in the early 1930's. Walking down Bond Street with my mother after an unsuccessful interview with a flower training school, we came to Atkinson's window. Many of you will, I feel sure, remember the beautiful flower arrangements that were displayed in these windows, but the one that really entranced me was an arrangement of leek seed-heads in a beautiful Egyptian urn. I knew at once that whoever made this had something that I must learn about. So off we went to find out and to be told that they were arranged by Constance Spry who then ran a small flower shop by the name of 'Flower Decorations' next door. With all the luck in the world I was allowed to start as an apprentice three months later.

From that day on I felt I could never work anywhere else and I was connected with Mrs Spry for the last 20 years of her life. In those years I never ceased to admire her, to look forward to every meeting, and to come away filled with a desire to create something fresh. Her knowledge on endless subjects made her a great conversationalist, full of fun, with a never ending fund of anecdotes and stories. Her ability to look ahead made her the greatest personality in the flower world. She had great artistic sensibility, and a gift for seeing the unusual. I shall always feel indebted to her.

After the war a very wonderful husband gave me all the encouragement and help I could have to carry on in the work I had come to love. The passing years brought a wealth of experiences which gave me a vast amount of pleasure and for which I feel deep gratitude as I look back at them. I had the honour of doing flowers for so many members of the Royal family and being so charmed by their interest in everything one did for them. There was the delight at being presented on two occasions to the Queen Mother—once at a charity fete at Hatfield and later at the Royal Show at Cambridge where I had helped with the flowers for the Royal Pavilion. Then the excitement of arriving next day to put the final touches to our arrangements in Westminster Abbey for the wedding of our present Queen and of driving through London at 6 a.m. cheered by the thousands of people who had stood all night along the route to catch just a glimpse of the bride. We stood like statues for five hours in the Abbey by permission of the Dean to watch the magnificent service and the pageantry, which I shall never forget. Nor shall I forget the radiance of the bride and the charm of the bridegroom.

Later I had a glimpse of the transformation of the City of Westminster schools for the luncheon given to all the Queen's guests on her Coronation Day. It was wonderful to be allowed the first glimpse of the present Duke of Kent as a baby of a day old while doing flowers outside the Duchess's bedroom. There were flowers for the Duke of Windsor at Fort Belvedere and being allowed to pick branches of silver birch, catkins and palms from the lovely woodland in that enchanting garden that looks over Virginia Water.

We arranged flowers for city banquets of such grandeur that it took one back hundreds of years. I can remember being spellbound by the gold plate and facinated by watching hundreds of legs of lamb turning on spits in the famous

Livery Hall kitchens. Those luscious cream cakes brought in by Mrs Spry and eaten ravenously with dirty hands after the late hours for rush jobs! Private banquets and parties. Derby night dinners for Lord Derby and table arrangements in his racing colours. Wonderful teas in the staff kitchens, and the vast underground world under Stafford House with its own butcher's shop. Debutante dances with the never-ending piano tuning, and one, two, three, four booming out as microphones were tested. A marquee at Ham House where we did hundreds of yards of garlands to link up with plaster masks and the decor of a very up and coming young man by the name of Oliver Messel, later to seek our assistance at many functions at the Opera House for gala nights and private parties.

We arranged flowers for shops and restaurants, and in many of London's beautiful churches, St. Margaret's, Westminster, Pont Street, All Saints, Langham Place and for the Duke and Duchess of Norfolk in Holy Trinity, Brompton. A wedding in St. Paul's Cathedral. Flowers for showrooms and films; my first introduction to the hours of waiting to get on sets. The realisation that film stars work so hard. The frustration of delays, and watching some pieces of films retaken as often as ten times until every small detail was correct. Walking round the plasterer's and carpenter's shops, visiting the reference library to ensure that every jewel in a hand-made sword for a member of a guard of honour seen in a film for a few minutes only was correct in shape and colour. Gowns and scenery checked and re-checked for authenticity.

A thousand memories crowd in. Taking large arrangements through London by taxi for a wedding where someone had overlooked the order. Being collected at 4 a.m. by van to be driven to the shop and help make the bouquets for the wedding of the Duchess of Gloucester. Driving to Brighton and having the lovely job of doing flowers for the opening of the Brighton Pavilion.

Through it all I have had the comradeship of the shop and my fellow workers: Mr Foss in particular with his never-ending help, Mr Spry, Mr Marr, Miss Oldfield, Miss Pirie, Mrs Dichie, Mrs Daphne, Gotto, Eleanor, Robbo, Jean, Watsie, Derby, Whitie, Viola, Bow, Ann and so many more.

The feeling of alertness by everyone the moment Mrs Spry appeared. To her I feel I owe so much.

I would also like to thank Mr G. R. Kingbourn for the delightful line drawings he took so much trouble to prepare for this book. I am also indebted to the Editor of *Housewife* who has very kindly allowed me to use some photographs which have appeared in that magazine.

These later years have brought the development of flower clubs and the changing pattern of many things. There has been teaching, lecturing and demonstrating to help so many people who want to do flowers for themselves—some people whose parties one might have done for them in pre-war days.

The love of flowers has no social barrier. I have travelled all over the British Isles, thousands of miles each year by car and train, making many good and lasting friends. There have been visits abroad, to Paris, Ceylon, all the capital cities of Australia on a fascinating tour recently.

Every day there was another flower, plant or shrub new to me to be learned about. The learning included various techniques on preservation of material, textures, colour blending, choice of containers and the hundred and one different things one has to know as a flower arranger—and I find I am still learning. I have enjoyed the honour of judging at many of our famous flower shows, not excluding Chelsea. All these things and many more have given me a wealth of experience and enjoyment, some of which I have tried to pass on to my readers in this book.

Vases and Containers

I must first deal with the most fundamental matter in flower arranging: the vase or container. Container has become the standard description as we so often use boxes, bowls, jugs, tins, pans, baskets and sundry other objects not designed to hold flowers. Mrs Constance Spry did much to open our eyes not only to the use of uncommon plant material but also to the value of novel containers.

Daffodils, marigolds, daisies, berries and many annuals look at their best in baskets or simple vessels of brass or copper. Tulips can be set in good china or glass.

In the summer there is such a profusion of flowers that the vessel becomes relatively less important, and the use of all manner of bowls, basins and ovenware dishes can give you just the effect which you require.

The flat dweller in town needs vases which are easily and economically filled with flowers. A lovely piece of Dresden or Chelsea china may only require the addition of a handful of primroses or a posy of the gentianella. Money spent on a really lovely vase can save you many shillings.

Boxes and baskets need containers for water. In the old days these were made to measure of zinc or lead and were quite an expensive item, but the method generally used now is to find a pudding bowl or pie dish that will fit the box or basket and will hold sufficient water for a reasonably large flower arrangement. The new metal foil containers used for pies and puddings can also be pressed into service.

How are the flowers to be kept in place in these vessels? My favourite method is to use crushed up wire-netting of 2-inch mesh. From Japan, the American flower arrangers took the Kenzan or needle point holder, and this aid to the placing of tall subjects in low, open containers is now obtainable here. Florapak, or Oasis, which is more solid and green in colour, are best held in place in the vase with a piece of wire-netting.

9

Camellia williamsii Citation

▲

◀ *Camellia japonica Elegans*

Camellias arranged with their own foliage

Waxy flowers and glossy leaves

Camellias are being more widely grown in this country now that people realise that they are not, as our Victorian ancestors wrongly thought, tender plants suited only to their beloved stove houses. The art of placing them in the garden is to be sure that they are not in a position where the early morning sun can reach them, for should this occur while the blossom are in the grip of overnight frost these will be scorched and unsightly. They do very well with a north or west aspect and may be used as under-shrubs in the dappled shade of small deciduous trees growing in acid soil.

When I was in Australia I spent a most interesting afternoon visiting the famous camellia garden of Mr Waterhouse where I saw many varieties which I had not seen before, the majority growing in tubs. Mr Waterhouse is the author of a wonderful book, *The Camellia Trail*, which has illustrations by the artist Paul Jones whom I had the pleasure of meeting.

I think you will find that many shrub nurseries here in Britain offer very good selections of camellias which, although they may seem expensive, will reward the purchaser with their beautiful dark green foliage and abundant blooms for many years. The foliage is excellent in winter flower arrangements and I am quite happy to have a vase containing nothing but these magnificent burnished leaves. I shall never forget the sight which I saw in Cornwall recently of the single white camellia called White Wings set against a grey stone wall.

The varieties of camellia used here are mostly hardy out-door kinds, many given to me by my dear friend the late Francis Hanger. How sorely we shall miss his patience and generosity, and his knowledge born of long experience. These camellias were all picked in March after a spell of very sharp frosty weather, but they opened well in water, even the very tightest buds.

I remember arranging in mid-winter a vase of camellia foliage. I cheated by fixing on the branches a few wax imitation blossoms, only to find that after several weeks in a hot London restaurant the real flower buds had opened. It was instructive to see that although the wax flowers had looked quite well without the real thing for comparison, they looked very tawdry beside the lovely, fragile, fresh blossoms, which had been rendered more delicate in colour by the forcing they had undergone.

◀ *Camellia japonica Mathotiana alba*

10

▲ *Garrya elliptica*

Grey Tassels and Grey-Green Leaves
Eucalyptus, Garrya elliptica and a cabbage

For this group I have used one of my favourite winter shrubs, *Garrya elliptica*, a Californian evergreen introduced by David Douglas, and named after Mr Michael Garry of the Hudson Bay Company who gave Douglas much assistance in his plant hunting and research in 1828. When cut the long, grey, catkins last well. The foliage may have to be removed, as wintry winds are apt to burn it. Each plant bears either male or female flowers but the male pollen-bearing plant is to be preferred as it has longer catkins. The grace and elegance of the pendulous catkins of the garrya in various stages of maturity are most welcome to the flower arranger as they give a good outline shape to any group in which they appear. Trees of garrya planted in the open garden with room to spread out take on a beautiful shape and I believe it is a mistake to grow this tree cramped against a wall as I, alas, have done.

With the garrya I have used branches of the lovely grey-leaved eucalyptus. You will find that the eucalyptus grows well in the garden once the first winter has been safely passed, sometimes putting on three feet of growth in a year. *E. populifolia* and *E. globulus* have good foliage, but the hardiest species is *E. gunnii*, the Cider Gum of Tasmania. If you cannot grow these leaves you may buy them at a florist, as they are imported annually from the South of France. *E. perriniana* is another hardy gum which produces very decorative young foliage if it is pruned fairly severely.

Lastly, the centre of interest in the group is provided by the decorative cabbage which, unlike the kale that we have used for many years, has an excellent solid heart. This plant is available in white and purple colouring, both of which are good. Seed may be sown in spring and thinned out in May or June to give good solid plants to cut for winter decoration. The decorative kales from seed are well worth space in the kitchen garden, although I have a friend who grows a few in front of a shrub border to give colour in the winter.

Though the use of these decorative vegetables may seem a new idea, if you study Japanese prints you will find that in fact they were so used hundreds of years ago in Japan.

◀ *Eucalyptus perriniana*

12

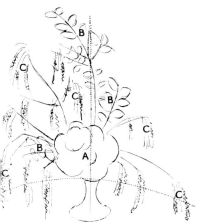

A.   *Cabbage*
B.   *Eucalyptus leaves*
C.   *Garrya elliptica*

Galanthus nivalis

Anemone blanda scythinica

Iris histrioides major

A Mixture of Spring Bulbs

Curious hermodactylus are blended with other bulbs

In this spring group there are some flowers of the more unusual spring bulbs in an elegant container which gives importance to the small, fragile-looking blooms. The mourning widow iris, *Hermodactylus tuberosus*, with its delicate lime green colour and black velvet, turned back petals is a little bulb rarely grown although the flowers have been sold in Covent Garden for the last 25 years.

Anemone blanda, used twice in the central axis of the arrangement, is a lovely rock garden plant giving shades of pink and blue in mid-February. It lasts well in water, unlike our sweet native wood anemone. You will see that I have used some crocus blooms. These are not the large-flowered Dutch hybrids, but some of the earlier and more delicate looking species and their varieties: my favourites are the pure white Snow Bunting, Cream Beauty with brilliant orange stamens and *Crocus tomasinianus* which has a range of delicate soft purple colouring. It is good to see these small flowers in the rock garden opening wide to the first blink of sun in early February.

I have used a large early flowering form of the snowdrop, *Galanthus nivalis maximus*, which has large grey green leaves.

Pale blue is supplied by the grape hyacinth, *Muscari azureum*, which has slightly smaller blooms than the more common varieties. A delicate yellow double narcissus, Primrose Cheerfulness, a sprig of forsythia and a few of the lovely blue *Iris histrioides major* complete the group. The black and white photograph cannot possibly do justice to the glorious blue of *Iris histrioides major*.

It was only recently that I realised that there are two distinct species; the one we have been dealing with, *I. histrioides* and *I. histrio*. *I. histrio* was grown by my grandmother, and thinking back and remembering those flowers, and comparing them with the plant I now have, *histrioides major*, I thought that some delightful delicate quality had been lost. I now understand very well that I was comparing two different, though closely related species. I have already praised *histrioides major*, but though it is quite lovely I think it is not so fine as its near relation. I believe that *histrio* is now so scarce as to be almost unobtainable. Both are, however, beautiful things; the bulbs increase readily, and the flowers will even appear unharmed through the snow of early February.

14

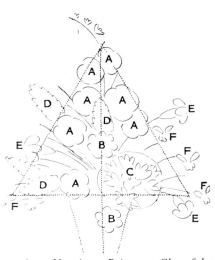

A.   *Narcissus Primrose Cheerfulness*
B.   *Anemone blanda*
C.   *Crocus species*
D.   *Muscari azureum*
E.   *Hermodactylus tuberosus*
F.   *Galanthus nivalis maximus*

Zantedeschia aethiopica

An Arrangement for February

Arum lilies and catkins

Lilies are flowers that I have grown to love through the years. As a child, I even disliked them. I have carried out the floral decoration of many a wedding and have learnt to appreciate the qualities of magnificence and grandeur of this luminous flower, so eminently suitable a subject to provide decoration on a great occasion.

Arum lilies, although not true lilies, have this same outstanding quality to an even greater degree, with an added suggestion of depth of texture approaching the softness of chamois leather.

A branch of hazel catkins, three arum lilies and three arum leaves form this design. This is a February arrangement that lasts well and has great charm. The arum lilies have had their thick, pliable stems bent by gentle massage into the required curves. Their solidity and gracefulness make the perfect foil for leafless branches of oak or pear encrusted with lichen, or well-shaped sprays of hazel, alder or poplar catkins. By completely submerging the arum leaves overnight in a very dilute starch solution they may be made to last for many days. This method is useful in church decoration where it is essential that the material lasts in good shape for several days without attention.

You will see that the flowers and leaves spring from a little Chinese bowl which is set upon a round stoneware dish. The flowers are supported by a pinholder which is hidden by a sprinkling of shingle. The shingle is repeated within the large dish, where it is used to reinforce the shadow.

Some years ago I came upon a hardy form of the arum lily growing and flowering in an unsheltered garden. Now at last I have obtained a plant and am impatiently awaiting the results.

Another lily I have grown recently is the Golden-rayed Lily of Japan, *Lilium auratum*. I bought some excellent bulbs from Woolworths and soaked them in wet peat for a few days before planting, which plumped them up. I then planted them deeply (as they produce roots on the stem above the bulb) in a mixture of sharp sand, leaf-mould and peat. They have grown to a height of four feet and to my delight have produced four or five huge blooms per stem. More commonly grown are the Madonna lily, the Tiger lily and *Lilium regale*, all excellent flowers as well as being first-class garden plants.

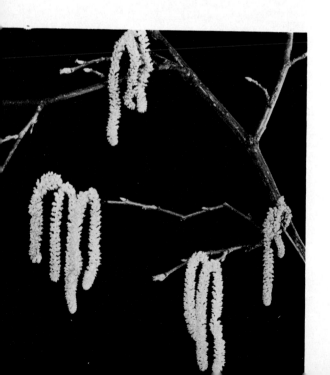

◀ *Corylus avellana, the common hazel*

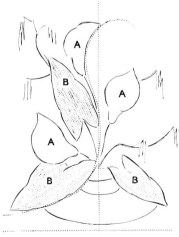

A.   *Arum lilies*
B.   *Arum leaves*

17

Pieris japonica

Corylopsis glabrescens

Mahonia japonica

Very Early Flowering Shrubs *Mahonia, lily of the valley tree and rhododendrons*

Many articles are to be found about early flowering shrubs in the gardening papers. Flowering shrubs, in fact, are fashionable and the vogue has not reached its climax yet.

The collection shown in this arrangement is made up of a number of shrubs, each of which has distinctive character, either of shape, elegance, colour or texture which fits it for inclusion.

Starting with the top of the group we find a stem of corylopsis, whose catkin-like flowers are of primrose yellow. This shrub flowers in January and February and not only is it a delight in the garden, but most useful to the flower arranger. One or two sprays add greatly to an early spring group, and moreover, they will fill the room with scent. It is fortunate that flowers do not set out only to please our eyes; for though one cannot achieve with the aid of plants such as honeysuckle and jasmine remarkable arrangements of subtle line and perfect symmetry, their exquisite fragrance more than compensates, and even when we cannot see them their sweet presence is made apparent throughout the whole room.

Then come flower spikes of the lily-of-the-valley tree, *Pieris japonica*, stripped of its leaves. This, like most ericaceous plants, needs an acid soil, and grows to perfection in Cornwall, loving both climate and soil. A spray of the variegated camellia comes next, giving solidity to the group, and adding a touch of yellow of that greenish tinge which is the only yellow that really blends with pink. Then there are a few flower heads of the early flowering hybrid rhododendron, Christmas Cheer. It does flower soon after Christmas and gives one a pleasant shock of suprise; but to have it early one must give it a really sheltered spot. The sweetly scented golden blossoms of *Mahonia japonica* are there, but without its spiny pinnate leaves. It is noticeable that mahonias grown in poor soil produce the best-coloured foliage.

You will also note a budded branch of camellia, a spray of dried heather flowers and finally some pieces of scented *Daphne mezereum* to give outline shape and also to add its subtle perfume to the bouquet.

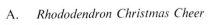

A. *Rhododendron Christmas Cheer*
B. *Pieris japonica*
C. *Mahonia japonica*
D. *Dried heather*
E. *Corylopsis*

19

Achillea Coronation Gold

Acanthus spinosus

Aucuba japonica variegata

Dried Material and Brilliant Lime Green Flowers

Cherry laurel, Bear's Breeches and hydrangeas

In the early spring tall flowers and foliage are scarce and one is forced to make use of dried material though perhaps with a feeling that this would be better on the bonfire. Even earlier, before Christmas in fact, I like to use dried seed-heads with chrysanthemums as I feel this delicate material is a better foil for these much-loved flowers than the solid-looking winter evergreens. This dried material can be given a new lease of life by adding a little fresh material.

I have used *Helleborus foetidus* here to give a beautiful central mass of emerald green. These elegant sprays of pendant, bell-shaped flowers are ideal not only because of their colour, but their solid shape is a foil for the flimsy delicacy of the seed-heads. The lower leaves are those of cardoon, a near relation of the globe artichoke, which many people overlook, but which is in constant use by experienced flower arrangers.

Cardoons can be grown from a spring sowing to produce strong plants by the autumn. The large, purple-blue thistle flowers can be used as well as the foliage. These globular heads when dried become the rich red-brown of a fox.

Returning to our flower arrangement, you will note variegated cherry laurel and variegated holly. When using solid large-leaved winter evergreens be sure to sponge the leaves and remove the dirt which would spoil their lovely glossy foliage. You will find that even in the country they become surprisingly grimy, especially after foggy weather. If you sponge this foliage with a little olive oil it imparts a fine gloss.

At the apex of the group you will find seed-heads of *Veratrum nigrum*, which follow the unusual black flowers. This herbaceous perennial plant would be worth growing for the sake of its fine leaf which looks as though it had been accordion pleated. Lastly, there is a dried flower spike of the acanthus, which has the extraordinary vernacular name, Bear's Breeches. When you dry this plant wait until the flowers are showing at the top of the spike, then when this has dried off you should place it in a little water for by this means the white flowers are rendered 'Everlasting' retaining their whiteness indefinitely.

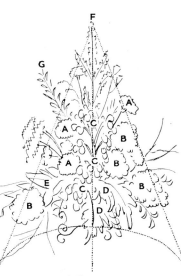

A. *Achillea*
B. *Dried hydrangea heads*
C. *Helleborus foetidus*
D. *Cardoon leaves*
E. *Aucuba leaves*
F. *Dried flowers of dock*
G. *Dried flowers of acanthus*

21

▲ *Helleborus orientalis*

The Joy of Winter Flowers

Christmas roses soften the angular Winter Sweet

What pleasure there is to be derived from shrubs and herbaceous plants sufficiently hardy to flower outdoors in winter! At one time I felt depressed at the thought of waiting years for shrubs to bloom with sufficient freedom to cut from them the stems needed to furnish a bowl, but experience has taught me how quickly those years pass and how worthwhile the results can be. As early as January the winter sweet, *Chimonanthus fragrans*, will unfurl its fragile, pale golden flowers, each with a rich red centre and so fragrant that they fill the air for yards around with their perfume. It has a stiff, angular habit of branching and it flowers long before the leaves appear, so in arrangements it needs the foil of something softer in outline and more leafy in texture. That is why, for this winter vase, I chose white Christmas roses, *Helleborus niger*, green hellebores, *H. foetidus*, and the shining dark green leaves of the Italian arum, *A. italicum*.

Hellebores of all kinds are, to me, a great joy and they can be grown quite easily from seed though it takes a little time. Colours range from the pure white of the Christmas rose, through all shades of green and purple to the intense, almost blackish maroon of some varieties of Lenton rose, *H. orientalis*. The common hellebore in this arrangement has emerald green flowers that stand well in water but some other kinds are not so easy and it is necessary to stand the stems in an inch of boiling water for several minutes and then give them a long drink. A special difficulty with the Christmas rose itself is that it starts to bloom on very short stems. A few handfuls of dry leaves or peat placed over each plant in November will help to lengthen the stems and make them more suitable for arrangement. A cloche over each plant also draws up the stems and keeps the flowers clean. Beware of slugs which relish these dainty buds.

The Italian arum is one of the best foliage plants I grow in my garden. In the open the exquisitely shaped leaves commence to unfold in late December and one can go on picking them until July when the whole plant dies down. I well remember my distraction the first summer I grew this plant and, after a dry spell, thought I had lost it altogether. Of course, it had only taken its natural rest.

◀ *Chimonanthus fragrans*

A. *Chimonanthus fragrans*
B. *Helleborus niger*
C. *Arum leaves*

Daffodils naturalised in a park

A group of trumpet daffodils

Daffodils and Bright Green Moss

Cork disguises an ovenware dish

The beloved daffodils present one of the most difficult problems to the flower arranger. I think this is partly owing to their stiff form and lack of substantial foliage; indeed they are often sold in bunches without any leafage at all. They look their best growing in grass. I think of Cambridge in the spring with the soft grey stone of the old colleges, the elegant trees reaching for the sky, and around their roots the clusters of sheer gold daffodils. This I feel is something everyone should see at least once in a lifetime.

One should try to interpret the natural growth in arranging this flower and the illustration shows the use of one bunch of twelve daffodils and some green bun moss sometimes obtainable from the florist. I have used two pieces of cork, one at the front and one at the back, to cover a very ordinary ovenware dish. The cork has an excellent texture and brings out the true quality of these flowers; it can be bought at many stores and florists' shops. For those who live in the country, pieces of natural bark are even more suitable for this purpose. Daffodils look well when arranged in a bed of moss set in a basket, a copper pan or some kind of wooden container. They become less expensive as the year advances and one can use them in generous quantities, arranging them with branches of spring foliage, but they need simple treatment; they are not for sophisticated arrangements.

Daffodils, unlike most other flowers, really last longer if placed in shallow water, and can be arranged in shallow dishes without fear that they will quickly wilt. I do feel that we should be grateful to the growers of daffodils for they produce them so early and so cheaply that I feel sure anyone would consider five shillings well spent on such a bunch as I used for this arrangement in early January.

Have you tried growing a dozen bulbs of daffodils in a bowl of shingle? This makes a change from bulb fibre and all the attention they require is water at regular intervals. Keep them in a dark cupboard for a few weeks and as soon as the green tips burst out bring them into full light. The shingle, which is that used on some greenhouse staging, can be bought from garden sundriesmen.

24

A. *Container and pinholder*

B. *Bark placed in position*

C. *The completed arrangement*

▲ *Viburnum opulus sterile*

Anticipating Spring

Golden forsythia, guelder roses, hyacinths and pussy willow

This is obviously a spring arrangement. However, I have made it expensively from flowers purchased from the florist in January, just to give a wonderful cheering arrangement on a dull winter day. You can, of course, wait until the flowers are available in the garden, and you will save a good deal of money, though you will not get the lift which my out-of-season flowers gave me.

The low, grey, square pottery dish is only partly occupied with flowers. For once I decided to let the water surface be visible to add its own sparkling contribution to the effect and it seemed to enhance the limpid vernal quality.

The narcissus used here is the bunch-flowered Geranium, in creamy-white with a vermillion cup and most sweet scent. The imported Dutch sprays of guelder rose are in that strange emerald white colour which they assume when forced. Sprays cut from your own trees in the spring will not have just that ethereal greenish hue. I have added a few florist's carnations whose pink colour combines with that of the other flowers to compose a pastel harmony.

The three stems of blue hyacinths were cut from a bowl of the bulbs when they had grown a little leggy, and they looked much better in the group than when languidly drooping over the edge of the bulb bowl. The great gain in using the hyacinth in arrangements is in having their strong, sweet scent which is simply poured out into the room. The scent of the hyacinth has for me a special charm, for it immediately takes me back in memory to happy childhood days with big bowls of hyacinths, log fires and buttered crumpets for tea.

You will see at the top left of this group a flowering branch of forsythia. This can be easily forced if you care to cut it when in bud and keep it in a warm room. You must allow quite three weeks for this operation but when the buds burst one is well rewarded by the cheerful golden flowers on the dark leafless stems. *Forsythia intermedia spectabilis* is perhaps the most vigorous form and certainly one of the most widely grown forsythias, but the more slender *F. suspensa* is worth growing on a wall or fence. It has pendant branches decked with blossoms of a paler yellow than *F. intermedia spectabilis*.

◀ *Salix caprea*

26

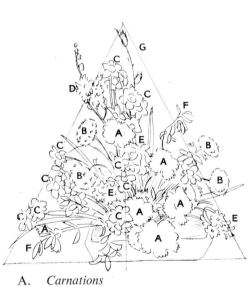

A. *Carnations*
B. *Viburnum opulus sterile*
C. *Narcissus Geranium*
D. *Forsythia*
E. *Hyacinth*
F. *Hazel catkins*
G. *Salix caprea* (*Willow palm*)

27

▲ *A double tulip*

A Modern Epergne

The charm of an all white arrangement

This two tiered arrangement of short-stemmed flowers is intended to give the atmosphere of a wedding. The flowers, which are all white, include double tulips, white hyacinths, freesias, *Pieris japonica*, *Viburnum opulus sterile*, and a few spikes of the lovely lily-of-the-valley, *Convallaria majalis*.

I have given the flowers all the gracefulness of arrangement possible in dealing with such short-stalked subjects, for this could very easily become a stiff and formal group, lacking all elegance and charm. Although in fact the arrangement was carefully studied, I think the flowers give the pleasing impression that they have naturally taken up the positions which they occupy. The formality is given at once in a wedding arrangement of this type by restricting the flowers to a candid whiteness.

The vase is a simple modern version of the Victorian epergne. As the two metal containers of which it is made up are not of any great beauty in themselves I had no scruples about allowing my flowers to conceal them. The white hyacinth is the one named L'Innocence. The solid-looking double white tulip is called Purity and the more shapely single-flowered ones are the mid-season Mendel tulip with the name White Sail. The freesias are white selected forms of the recently introduced giant-flowered variety and, with the forced lily-of-the-valley sprays and the hyacinth, add the attraction of sweet fragrance to this chaste arrangement. The *Pieris japonica*, sometimes called lily-of-the-valley tree, is a very useful evergreen for those whose gardens are not on chalk soil. I grow in addition *Pieris formosa forrestii* which has cockcombs of brilliant scarlet new growth in the early part of the year quite as bright as any flower; later the white sprays of flowers appear to give a second period of beauty to this very fine but rather tender shrub.

The epergne, which generally had a complicated system of branching flower holder, was essentially a centrepiece to dominate any subsidiary floral arrangement that the table might have. This type of vase is useful in the arrangement of roses, especially those with slender stems which may be set to cascade gracefully outward and downward. I am fond of an arrangement of clashing reds. The discord of magenta, crimson and orange is stimulating and cheering, especially for a party or dining table.

◀ *Convallaria majalis*

A.   *Double white tulip, Purity*
B.   *Mendel tulip, White Sail*
C.   *White hyacinth, L'Innocence*
D.   *Viburnum opulus sterile*
E.   *White freesias*
F.   *Pieris japonica*
G.   *Lily-of-the-Valley*
H.   *Ivy fruits*

Polyanthus

Hamamelis mollis

Erica carnea

A Medley of Spring Flowers

Witch hazel, winter-flowering heather and roman hyacinths

How one longs to use the delightful flowers of spring, and especially the flowering bulbs. Their use in arrangements, however, presents two problems: their stalks are short and they have very little foliage.

The picture shows spring flowers in a bed of moss, which looks appropriate and has the added advantage of concealing the crushed 2-inch wire-netting which holds the flowers in place. The outline shape is given by the naturally lovely branches of the witch hazel, *Hamamelis mollis*, a shrub which provides in mid-February an abundance of yellow flowers on branches of truly Chinese elegance.

Heathers are a joy to use in winter flower decorations and the winter-flowering varieties of *Erica carnea* will all grow well, even on a limestone or chalk soil, though most heathers demand an acid soil. These heathers look well if planted in the front of the shrub border, and here with selection you may have heathers in bloom all year. Their great value for cutting, however, is when other flowers are scarce.

The primulas, including *Primula* Wanda and the polyanthus, give with their strong colours a central focal point in the flower group illustrated. I feel that some touches of blue and yellow are almost essential in mixed flower arrangements and here the blue is given by the cluster of grape hyacinths on the right.

In the lower left hand corner of the group opposite you will see the flowers of the useful but *very* invasive winter heliotrope, petasites. In flower arrangements the winter heliotrope has many good qualities which must be set against its weediness in the garden: it lasts well in water; it will scent a whole room and its admittedly dull pink flowers are good in texture and helpful when one is blending pink and yellow flowers.

In the central front a small spray of the stinking hellebore, *Helleborus foetidus*, gives a brilliant touch of lime green. I grow this hellebore from seed and place the plants among my shrubs where their strange, lovely green blossoms flourish in the overhead shade of the taller plants.

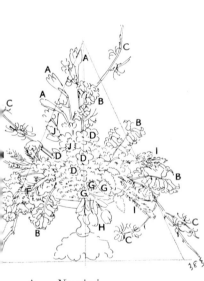

A.   *Narcissi*
B.   *Roman hyacinths*
C.   *Chinese Witch Hazel*
D.   *Primula polyanthus varieties*
E.   *Chaenomeles speciosa*
F.   *Petasites fragrans (Winter*
                     heliotrope)
G.   *Muscari (Grape hyacinth)*
H.   *Helleborus foetidus*
I.   *Erica carnea*
J.   *Shrubby veronica*

31

Darwin tulips

Lily-flowered tulips

Viridiflora tulips

Contrasting Tulip Shapes

Apple blossom and striped, splashed and frilly-edged tulips

Two branches of apple blossom help to emphasise the composition of this vase of tulips. To get the greatest interest from an arrangement of these fine flowers it is well to have blooms in various stages of freshness. When the tulip first takes on its colour it is a very stiff upright flower, but when left in water for a few days the stems soften, take on better lines and generally become much more adaptable for arranging.

You will see that the line flows from left to right. To obtain the balance of this type of design you must be most careful that the height on the left corresponds nearly to the same extent as the lower flower or branch on the right. In this case it happens to be the two stems of apple blossom that give the outline shape and are in consequence a very important feature of this arrangement. The vase, a dolphin, lends itself well to this shape and design having a good size bowl at the top of an elegant stem.

I have mixed several forms and varieties of tulip which are interesting to me: the lily-flowered tulip with its slender pointed petals; the *viridiflora* tulip, a very unusual flower, striped green and yellow; the black tulip used to give contrast (it can add character to an arrangement of pink tulips); the little frilly edged tulip, Sundew, in bright cerise; some Rembrandt striped and splashed tulips; and, finally, as a centre of interest, a large double May-flowering tulip.

Tulips are quite one of the best of all cut flowers and if you choose your varieties you can have an almost continuous blooming season of four months. In early spring there are the brilliant scarlet kaufmannianas which often flower in February, followed by the early doubles, cottage and Rembrandt types, to late peony-flowered doubles which continue until nearly June. They are quite the greatest value for money. They are better lasters than the average daffodil as a cut flower though the bulbs do not have quite the same quality as daffodils for increasing to give years of pleasure in the garden. Normally they are removed from the ground and stored, but I have found they bloom quite well a second year if allowed to stay in the ground. Tulips have enough of their own foliage to complete an arrangement without the use of any unrelated material.

A. *Double tulip*
B. *Apple blossom and leaves*

33

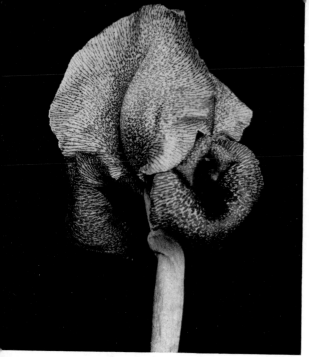

▲ *Iris susiana*

Flowers of Late Spring

Striped irises and streaked tulips

For this late spring arrangement I have chosen an upright vase to give a feeling of elegance. The lilac with its multitude of small flowers provides a foil for the more solid parrot tulips and the grey-blue iris. You will see that I have removed the foliage from the sprays of mauve lilac, as this reduces the transpiration. This is a useful tip when flowers with woody stems are used. You may also help the plant to absorb water more readily by hammering the stems and sinking them deeply in water prior to using them; or you may dip the ends of the branches in boiling water and then allow them a good long drink. A few sprays of the Preston hybrid add their grace to any vase, and pervade the room with a delicate scent rather like that of the privet flower. The correct name for these lilacs is *Syringa prestoniae* and one of my favourites is called Isabella which has long tentacles of mellow purple flowers. Though they give a lovely effect in the garden, after great efforts I have not found a way to make them last so that they are a really good cut flower. I feel three days in water is just about as long as I can hope to keep them. It is sad as even the newer and selected varieties of lilacs last very well once the foliage is removed and though this may be a disappointment to many people you can always add an extra stem of plain foliage.

The parrot or dragon tulips are beautiful but rather neglected flowers and a few bulbs are well worthy of a corner of your garden. The one used here is of a beautiful lilac colour, streaked as if by the brush of an artist with a darker shade of lilac. The grey and black veined and netted iris has a beautifully velvety texture, and the whole arrangement has a hazy greyish-purple effect which embraces also the dark lilac blue vase in a harmony of form and colour. Iris susiana belongs to the Regelio-cyclus section and needs very special care in the average flower garden. As they come from the East they need and enjoy being baked in very hot sun and given light soil, good drainage, plenty of sunshine and some bonemeal they should do well. They are quite exquisite with their large sombre heads and magnificent blending colours to add to many a cut flower arrangement.

◀ *Semi-double lilac*

A. *Parrot tulips*
B. *Irises*
C. *Lilac*
D. *Rose*

35

▲ *Grandiflorus gladioli*

A Mid-Summer Arrangement

Plume poppy, fluffy thalictrum and delicately flushed roses

Having mentioned earlier the importance of a focal point, I feel that this picture will show another example of the principle which I have explained. The roses here form a solid central mass which is extremely important to the whole group. If you put your fingers over these and hide them from view you will understand, I think, what I mean. You are left with a good outline shape but a lot of confused bits and pieces of seed heads and branches which are quite without formal significance.

Among these flowers you will see some flowering stems of that light and feathery plant well named Plume Poppy, which the experts now ask us to call *Macleaya cordata*, not bocconia, though it will still be found as bocconia in the plant catalogues. When picked before it reaches maturity, it is as florists say, 'soft', which means that it tends to droop when cut and put in water. The very early branches of beech have this unfortunate quality of 'softness'. If you have patience and pick these somewhat later they will have matured and will last well in the cut stage.

I have also used a stem of a yellow gladiolus and several apricot carnations; the latter are used because of their colour which blends with lime greens and yellows. Next come two pieces of *Thalictrum speciosissimum* with soft yellow fluffy heads and excellent grey-green foliage, and I grow it more for the sake of these leaves than for its flowers. Other important elements in the group are the four flat umbels of yellow achillea, whose small clustered flowers are of a good sulphur yellow. These achillea flowers are valuable to the flower arranger as they not only last well, which is rather rare in a summer flower, but they also dry quite well and so are useful for at least seven months of the year, being especially good in adding colour to a winter arrangement of seed heads. These flat flower heads of achillea are also particularly useful as they provide a good focal point.

To come back to a consideration of the elements of composition with which this chapter started; you will note that the apex of this roughly triangular group, being not immediately over the container but slightly to the left, I have had to compensate by giving a little more weight to the material which sweeps downward and forward on the right.

◀ *Macleaya cordata*

A. *Hybrid tea roses*
B. *Achillea*
C. *Plume poppy*
D. *Gladiolus*
E. *Carnations*
F. *Thalictrum speciosissimum*

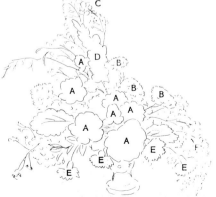

▲ *Lathyrus latifolius*

Peonies and Lime Flowers

Different lighting changes the arrangement

Peonies lend themselves to large flower groups better than any flower I know. There is a bold quality in their flat blowsy blooms which makes them suitable for the centre of a vase to give it solidity and character. Five or six blooms of this sort will give a focal point to any large arrangement. Heads of hydrangea have the same value; so also have blooms of dahlia, rose and the larger composite (daisy type) flower heads. When looking at an arrangement the eye quite naturally tends to seek the centre first, hence the great importance of seeing that this place is occupied by something of particular solidity and interest. This rule applies also to colour, for if you wish a blue colour to predominate it must occupy the heart of the arrangement. Your colour effects will gain much if you mass the flowers of each particular shape or tint instead of scattering small touches of various colours, which reduces and dissipates the impact, the resulting impression upon the eye being a mixture of the different hues. In designing vases of flowers in the traditional colours, red, white and blue, for the Queen's Coronation we had to bear in mind this matter of massing each colour in a solid block, for only in this way could be achieved the impression we required.

In this picture a silhouette effect is obtained by placing the vase on a ledge so that the main part of the group comes between us and the window. This gives a refreshing change as the effect is quite unlike that of the normal frontal illumination. The branches of lime flowers with broad leaves removed give a tracery effect and the whole arrangement looks light and delicate.

In a silhouette design of this kind colour is relatively less important than form, but the fact that leaves and petals are translucent adds much to the interest of this type of display.

At the base of this flower arrangement you will see blooms of the very useful everlasting pea, *Lathyrus latifolius*, which is one of the few perennial climbing plants. The only disadvantage to this pea is that it is quite without scent, which is apt to disconcert those who mistake the flowers for those of the fragrant annual sweet pea.

◀ *Peony Sarah Bernhardt*

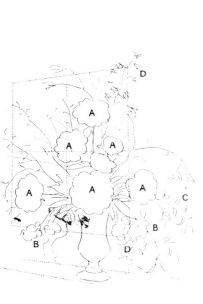

A. *Chinese peonies*
B. *Lathyrus latifolius*
C. *Lime flowers*
D. *Plume poppy flowers*

▲ *Fritillaria imperialis*

Soft Pinks and Yellows in May

Quaint shapes are blended together

My picture opposite was taken in May. The colour combination of soft pink and shades of yellow was interesting and unusual. You will see that the group is made up largely of solid, heavy looking flowers such as amaryllis, arum, crown imperial (*Fritillaria imperialis*). There are also two sprigs of golden gorse and some striking foliage of arum and bergenia.

The crown imperial is the pale yellow form, though there is an excellent range of bronze and gold colours in these magnificent flowers. I know a small cottage garden in Suffolk where these plants thrive; they have taken charge of at least thirty square yards, having the conditions they really do enjoy. I find it is well worth a detour in the car just to see the crown imperials, if I am within ten miles, as I have never seen them more at home. I, personally, never have a great deal of success as somehow my plants get attacked by the slugs in early spring and from then on they never have a chance.

I wonder if you know the legend connected with the crown imperial? The story is told that when Christ walked in the garden of Gethsemane that Eastertide many years ago, the crown imperial lilies proudly held up their heads, but have since felt humbled and ashamed, and now hang their heads with a teardrop in each eye. The teardrop is there to be seen if you invert the delicate bell-shaped flowers.

The central erect flower with the prominent club-like spadix is the yellow marsh plant *Lysichitum camtschatcense*, and below this a bloom of the tender yellow arum, *Zantedeschia elliottiana*, completes this rather exotic group.

The pale arum is not, of course, a hardy plant at all. The lysichitum on the other hand is a bog or water plant, growing well and being a most attractive early-flowering water lover. It is nice as a cut flower and it often plays a most important part in our Chelsea flower arrangements as it is an excellent shape and mixes well with a variety of colours from purples to oranges and yellows, and it is out generally just at the right time, the end of May.

Solid leaves at the base of this arrangement add weight and texture; had one used something more delicate it would have changed the entire character.

◀ *Lysichitum camtschatcense*

A. *Amaryllis*
B. *Crown Imperials*
C. *Lysichitum camtschatcense*
D. *Zantedeschia elliottiana*

Dianthus barbatus

A 17th Century Flower Picture

Poppies, sweet williams, foxgloves and lupins

Here in living flowers is a modern version of a Dutch flower piece. It is as well when arranging such a group to keep as close as possible to the restricted list of flowers from which the Dutch artists had to compose their lovely paintings. You may be rather surprised if you study the old flower pictures carefully to note that flowers of different seasons are brought together. They were, of course, painted from separate careful studies made previously when each plant was in flower.

The poppies are from a collection of Sutton's Art Shades. These perennial poppies are easily raised from seed, and decorate the garden as well as serving as material for such arrangements as this. They have a strangely hand-painted appearance, enhanced by a striking blotch of darker colour at the base of the petals which radiate from a central fluffy mass of stamens. Their off-beat colours are quite delightful and most useful to the flower arranger. These flowers need to have their stems dipped in boiling water to prolong their life, and picking them while they are in bud also helps, as they open out very well in water. The foxgloves also I grew from Sutton's seed from which in addition to the normal pink colour I had plants in lemon and apricot hues. At the top centre you will see some bearded irises, which though they are now obtainable in a very big range of colour were known to the Dutch in the original blue and purple range. One of my favourites is Silver City, a soft grey-blue shade; another in this group is in a combination of maroon and mustard colour which I find useful to aid in blending certain colour mixtures.

The seventeenth century Dutch were appreciative of any flower with a striking pattern of contrasting colour; and here I have, in my modern Dutch group, used auricula-eyed sweet williams, which like the poppies and foxgloves, I raised from seed. I do not suggest that a framed group of this sort would be a suitable everyday method of using flowers, but as a rather special party piece it could be very appropriate.

The picture frame can be either hung from a beam or it may be used for framing an alcove. For the best effect set the vase back slightly.

◀ *Lupins*

A. *Annual poppies*
B. *Bearded irises*
C. *Foxgloves*
D. *Clematis*
E. *Roses*
F. *Lupin*
G. *Sweet Williams*

43

Magnolia grandiflora — *Rose Perfecta* — *Rose Peace*

Two Simple Rose Arrangements

Skeletonised magnolia leaves and a gold lacquer tea caddy

What can one add in praise of this flower, so much used, so much enjoyed, and so much loved by every-one in all parts of the world and by people in all walks of life. All over England in gardens large and small, and in parks and public places one finds roses. Because of their almost continuous blooming during summer and autumn they are becoming ever more popular plants for the small garden. I sometimes regret that we can now get from the florist, forced roses in the depths of winter; it seems to reduce these precious summer flowers to the status of so much drapery.

The extremely simple group illustrated (top) is arranged in a large old black and gold lacquer tea caddy, a pie dish being used as a container for water. I think it makes a refreshing change in a book with so many groups of mixed flowers to see a simple vase containing blooms and leaves of one type of plant, in this case the hybrid tea rose. One reason for using a mixed arrangement is that one can usually find bits and pieces to pick without spoiling the general garden picture.

Roses, however, bloom in such profusion that they can be picked in some quantity without ill effect to plant or garden.

The hybrid tea roses used in this arrangement are some blooms and buds of Tiffany and Perfecta and two fully developed flowers of Charles Mallerin, whose rich velvety red colour is the darkest I know; it is in fact almost black in the shadows. Here it is used to give depth, an important point in an arrangement which is solely confined to one type of flower. Contrast also is obtained, and this is essential when you have limited your choice of flower, and cannot call upon the different forms and textures so useful in a group of mixed flowers and foliage.

My lower flower group has five full blown specimens and two buds of the ubiquitous Peace accompanied by some cream-coloured-skeletonised leaves of magnolia. These are real leaves treated in such a way that only the vascular system remains. They are made abroad for sale in this country, but the skeletonising of any stout leaves may be done by anyone who cares to enquire into the method.

44

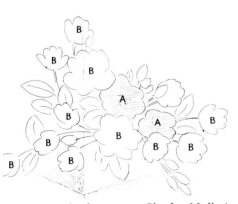

A. *Hybrid tea rose, Charles Mallerin*
B. *Hybrid tea roses, Tiffany and Perfecta*

A. *Hybrid tea rose, Peace*
B. *Skeleton leaves of magnolia*

Rosa alba Celeste

Favourite Old-Fashioned Roses

Sweet-scented jasmine, roses Céleste and Maiden's Blush

In turning from the modern rose to the beloved sweet-scented roses of the past I should like to quote the words written by Graham Thomas in his *Manual of Shrub Roses:* 'These roses were the favourites of the 18th and 19th century gardeners and reached the greatest perfection of their unique floral style around 1800. Their scent is proverbial, nothing in the garden or out of it is sweeter. They are double with masses of petals making a flower of camellia-like perfection, and with colours that the hybridists are busily trying to recapture to-day. They have the vigour of the wild species coupled with a richness that needs to be seen to be believed'. In these words you have a perfect picture of the old shrub roses. I don't think I can look at one without a pang as they are a constant reminder to me of Constance Spry. If ever she had favourite flowers I think surely it must have been the old roses which she grew with such pleasure and care, and loved so much.

When making your choice of roses do not overlook the old moss roses; they have a perfume all of their own and are hard to beat, especially just as the buds open out.

I think that for the small modern garden they have two disadvantages: first, that they are mostly large sprawling bushes difficult for the suburban and town gardener to cope with; secondly, most of them have really only one season of blooming, which many people resent, though strangely, they don't expect any other flowering shrub to give them more than one blooming in a season.

The little vase shown here might be suitable for use on a coffee table or in a guest's bedroom, or, as here, at the side of a writing desk. The advantage of sweet scent is most appreciated in a small vase which will be at close quarters.

Simplicity is the keynote of this country bunch which consists of a few sprays of sweet-scented jasmine and two very old country roses—Céleste and Maiden's Blush, both of which have a very sweet scent and pale pink colour. Céleste has one of the sweetest buds I know, quite perfect in its early stages, then opening out into a full blown rose, but only lasting a day or so. None of the old roses lasts really very well in water but I do find that all the buds open in a vase and so it is better to pick a mixture of roses at different stages of maturity and replace each one as it fades.

Jasminum officinale

46

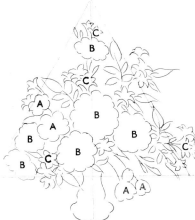

A. *Rosa alba Céleste*
B. *Rosa alba Maiden's Blush*
C. *Jasminum officinale*

▲ *Philadelphus speciosus*

Party Flowers

Apricot foxgloves, lilies and the magnificent yucca

Now I shall deal with party flowers, as these are most important on such occasions. Flowers can transform even a dreary wartime Nissen hut. I remember how one of our girls serving in the A.T.S. achieved a wonderful effect in this difficult art. She collected as many bicycle baskets as she could lay her hands on, fitted each with several jam jars to hold the water and then hung them round the walls. She then persuaded the willing villagers to contribute all the wild or garden flowers they could find and changed that dreary hall into a gay and attractive setting for a dance.

One important point about flower arrangements of this kind is that vases should be placed well out of reach; if possible above head level. For wedding receptions and cocktail parties this is extremely important as nearly all the guests will be standing and flowers placed on a side table, chest or bureau will be quite obscured from view.

In the left-hand picture on page 50 you see a group of flowers so arranged as to completely cover the low dish in which they are placed. This set upon a high tallboy was, I found, quite sufficient to decorate a large room for a dance given in a private house. The room was in shades of greys and pale pinks, the walls being dove grey and the glazed chintz curtains had a traditional flowery pattern in lovely pinks and greens on a background of grey which was somewhat darker in shade than the walls. It was early July, a time of flower abundance, and I was able to pick up the colourings of the room with the colourings of the blossoms.

In this group you will see spikes of foxgloves. These are the pale glowing blooms of Sutton's apricot tints which are so worthy of a shady spot in the garden. Sutton's have other varieties too, including a pale lemon coloured form. These may well be raised from seed to flower the year after sowing. The background twiggy growth on either side consists of sprays of lime blossoms in palest green, the long-stemmed, heart-shaped leaves having been removed. I have also defoliated the branches of the single-flowered philadelphus (wrongly called syringa) as this gives much more prominence to the pure white, strongly scented flowers set so gracefully on the dark brown stems. Included in this group you will note spikes of the American delphiniums called Pacific Hybrids. In this case I chose flowers of a true lilac-grey with a lovely muted quality which suited the indoor setting in which I placed it, as it picked up the greys of the walls and draperies. The clematis used is the hybrid

◀ *Excelsior foxgloves*

called Nellie Moser which has pale mauve flowers, each division being centrally banded with pink. I find that clematis need careful treatment to prolong their life as cut flowers. The method of dipping the tips of the stems in boiling water and then letting them have a good drink in a deep vessel is effective. It is important not to let the flowers come in contact with the boiling water or they will quickly become transparent.

I have used a number of flowers of the shell pink peony Solange to give solidity and substance to the group. The treatment of peonies to be used as cut flowers is strangely unlike that given to other subjects, for these useful flowers should actually be left without water for a period of about twelve hours, preferably resting on a cool stone floor. It is quite difficult for the flower lover to bring herself to do this, but it does prolong the life of the flower. The stems become dry with the treatment and must then be hammered and placed in water. I am told that in France where peonies are grown for market they are cut and left on the ground overnight, to be bunched, packed and transported next day. This means that when they arrive at Covent Garden they have been quite without water for some days. However, when you buy them and place them in a deep bucket of water they open out and seem to outlast those taken straight from the garden.

In my picture on page 51 you will see a large pedestal arrangement which was quite important enough when placed in the corner of a room to furnish the whole room—at least as far as flowers were concerned. The urn was of frosted glass and the pedestal base, encircled by a snake, was in a lovely shade of blue.

The unusual rounded bell-shaped blossoms used here are those of the yucca, a statuesque plant with sword-like spine-tipped leaves. I placed their thick stems in warm water for some hours prior to using them and they looked fresh and happy for three weeks. You will see that, as in the first group, I have again composed the background of flowering and defoliated lime branches. The hydrangea flowers are also leafless. *Lilium longiflorum* and the lily-like *Crinum capense* complete this group of party flowers in which I have kept green colour to a minimum.

The basket on the wall shown in the right-hand picture on page 50 is suitable for any party and here it is filled with flowers from the hedgerow and long sprays of rambler roses.

▲ *Lilium longiflorum*

Yucca flaccida ▶

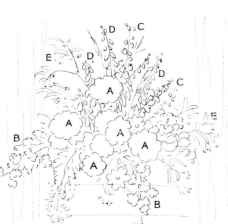

A. *Hybrid peony*
B. *Philadelphus*
C. *Delphinium*
D. *Foxgloves*
E. *Lime flowers*

A. *Elder flowers*
B. *Rambler roses*

50

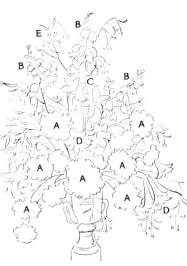

A. *Hydrangea*
B. *Yucca flowers*
C. *Crinum lilies*
D. *Lilium longiflorum*
E. *Lime flowers*

▲ *Gerbera jamesonii hybrids*

Barberton Daisies in a Beautiful Shell

A small-leaved ivy completes the arrangement

The gerbera forms the chief ingredient in this very simple arrangement. It is a native plant of South Africa and is sometimes called the Barberton or Transvaal daisy. In New Zealand it is a great favourite, and it was from that country that a Frenchman, Monsieur Maire, brought back a very varied collection with a range of fine colours. By further cultivation the range was extended to give about fifty distinct colour forms including white, cream, orange, apricot, salmon, reds of several types, maroon and every possible tint and shade of pink. Blues are not found in this range.

As cut flowers I have used them for many years, but only recently has there been such a fine range of large, handsome blooms to select from and they now join the list of flowers which we can obtain form the florist all the year round. If you wish to grow gerberas you will have to give them the greenhouse treatment needed by tender perennials, for this is the class to which these lovely daisies belong. Like all florist's flowers, their price fluctuates from season to season and round about Christmas time you will have to pay three shillings for a single bloom. The flowers will last, however, for at least three weeks in water.

You will note long sprays of the neat-growing, small-leaved ivy called *Hedera helix conglomerata*. I have it growing well on my rock garden. The brown coloured, rough-textured sprays of *Hippophae rhamnoides*, commonly known as Sea Buckthorn, set off the gerberas. The beautiful grey foliage of the Sea Buckthorn makes this shrub a joy for the flower arranger and it is particularly lovely when it is clustered with orange-yellow berries.

The vase is formed of a natural shell with an appropriate base and because of its charming patterned surface I have not concealed it more than I found necessary. It is rather important that the vase in a simple, intimate arrangement of this kind should be able to stand close inspection. You will realise that my few Barberton daisies might quite well be replaced by other flowers such as dahlias, carnations, roses etc., in fact just what is available at the florist's at the time you need them; or if you are so fortunate you may be able to select your few special blooms from your own garden.

◀ *Hedera helix conglomerata*

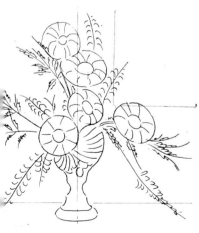

53

▲ *Passiflora caerulea*

Where Autumn Blends with Winter

The curious, trailing passion flowers

This is my favourite type of flower arrangement, and the materials of which it is composed are precious to me as they were all grown in my garden. I have aimed at suggesting the 'mellow fruitfulness' of the lovely autumn season in the small intimate group of passion flowers, grapes, roses, corn and *Viburnum fragrans*.

The container is also one for which I have great affection, and which I find I am constantly using in spite of the fact that I have a cupboard whose shelves are crowded with an assortment of vases of varied shapes, colours and sizes. I feel sure that most flower arrangers find that though they have a collection of vessels to select from, time and again the same favourite vase is used. I am also sure, however, that it is a mistake not to ring the changes, for if you change the container this will call for a new flower arrangement and you will find that you have transformed the whole appearance of your room; a refreshing thing to do occasionally. The particular vase which you see here is of ormolu and was given to me recently by great friends as a gift from Paris.

The small round grapes are from an outdoor vine which my mother gave me when first we came to our cottage. It is the strawberry grape whose fruits have a slightly strawberry-like flavour. As I find them rather disappointing to eat I use the delicate little bunches exclusively for their considerable decorative value. The passion flower is *Passiflora caerulea*, the only one of these lovely climbing plants of Brazil which is really hardy in my garden, growing on a south wall, where it provides an almost constant supply of its very remarkable blooms. A good covering of peat round the base of a passion flower creeper helps to keep the cold out and is very beneficial while the creeper is establishing itself. It is very tempting to cut away the rather straggly sprays as soon as flowering is over but leave this pruning until the spring because although they may look dead you will be surprised how often new growth springs from seemingly dead wood.

The sprays of *Viburnum fragrans* are, as the name suggests, scented. It is a hardy shrub that really comes to its best in the dead time of winter when the pinkish-white blossoms on the bare wood are a most cheerful sight.

◀ *Viburnum fragrans*

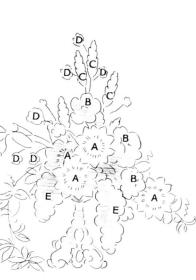

A. *Passion flowers*
B. *Hybrid tea roses*
C. *Wheat ears*
D. *Viburnum fragrans*
E. *Strawberry grape*

Phlox rosea superba   *Delphinium Ruth Langdon*   *Lilium regale*

A Basket of Summer Flowers *Tall herbaceous plants look well massed together*

In this basket is a mixture of summer flowers, mostly herbaceous perennials; plants which are at their best when massed generously. In a show there sometimes appears a class for a group representing 'Summer Glory' or 'Summer Profusion'. The arrangement illustrated here is, I think, just such a rich flowery multitude of summer beauties. Here is a chance to make use of flowers of many types with a great variety of form, colour and texture.

For a spring flower arrangement a basket often seems the most appropriate container, and looks particularly well with simple flowers such as daffodils, marigolds, daisies and wallflowers, whose colour, scent and profusion give such pleasure that no elaborate grouping is called for. I find that with such a group it is as well to cut out any faded flower and replace it with a fresh bloom.

Summer flowers such as we have in this arrangement do not last long in water but at least they fade gracefully and by constant topping up of the water level the arrangement will last well enough. Once you take such a group apart for re-

arrangement the petals will be shed and there will be little of any decorative value to retrieve. It is very much better to leave the flowers undisturbed for as long as there is any beauty left in them.

In my summer basket you will see: the Regal lily, delphinium, verbascum or mullein, phlox, achillea, antirrhinum or snapdragon, jasmine, thalictrum, roses and hydrangea. You will see that I have put into practise the rule about grouping each kind of flower to accentuate the form and colour and avoided a merely spotty effect.

Lilium regale, though it is new enough not to be found in the older books on lilies, has proved to be a most excellent garden plant which does not demand the care and trouble which deters many from growing lilies. This lily needs good drainage, and should be deeply planted to allow stem rooting to take place above the bulb level. Given a little patience, the three years needed to grow flowering bulbs from seed will be repaid by the possession of much healthier stock than can be obtained by quicker (and more expensive) means.

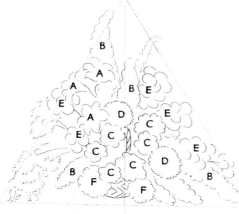

A. *Regal lilies*
B. *Delphinium*
C. *Hybrid tea roses*
D. *Achillea*
E. *Phlox*
F. *Hydrangea*

Sedum maximum atropurpureum

Sedum spectabile

Amaranthus caudatus

The Red Ink Plant

A study in form

I think that the use of unusual material adds to the interest of a flower arrangement. We have long since come to the end of the possiblities of combining all the commonest flowers, and so we turn to seeds, fruit and striking foliage to give variety to our arrangements.

In this group I have used the clustered blackish-red fruits of *Phytolacca americana*, the Red Ink Plant, to provide the dominant feature with its bold form. The fruits are at first green and then pass through red to reach their final colour which is that of a ripe blackberry, a rare and unusual hue very valuable to give contrast to pale colours, and quite dramatic when used with white material. Phytolacca was new to me until just after the war when I saw it in a Suffolk nursery. I wrote to enquire for it but was told that it was not available as their stock was depleted. However, some years later I was given seed by Mr Lugg of St. Albans and to my delight it germinated well and now sows itself about the garden giving me a stock of plants from whose corn-like roots the plants renew themselves each spring in the manner

of a dahlia; and like that plant they are cut down by the first frost. I must in fairness warn you that if the fruits fall on white clothing they will leave red stains.

I have also used the flowers of two stonecrops—*Sedum maximum atropurpureum* which has greenish flowers and strong purple leaves and, in the centre of the group, *Sedum spectabile* Autumn Joy, salmon-rose and bronze. I find these two stonecrops most serviceable in late summer as they last well in water, and have a solidity of substance.

The very large flower heads of hydrangea stand me in good stead at all stages of their development and here they blend with the general colour scheme of reds and pinks. Several of the forms of this mop-head hydrangea will colour well in the autumn.

Here also you will see the long, pendant flowers of Love-Lies-Bleeding, *Amaranthus caudatus albiflorus*. There are both red and green forms of this useful large-growing annual plant but the green stage of the so-called white form is the one which I find most helpful.

A. *Sedum blossoms*
B. *Phytolacca americana*
C. *Hydrangea flowers*
D. *Amaranthus caudatus albitlorus flowers*

▲ *Angelica archangelica*

Cow Parsley from the Hedgerows

Bold leaves and contrasting flower heads

Simplicity is sometimes the outstanding characteristic of a really successful flower arrangement. I can remember that on one occasion I went in a panic to my adviser in times of trouble, Mrs Spry. 'They want me to give a talk on advanced flower arrangement,' I said. She thought for a while, and then said 'Well it seems to me that the more advanced you are the more simple you become,' Later I thought this over and came to the conclusion that there was a lot of truth in it.

In this connection I am reminded of two weddings, where I had the fun of helping with the floral decorations. At St. Margaret's, Westminster, I decorated with the aid of the common white cow parsley of the hedgerows, placed in two large white urns. The effect was quite beautiful, as the lacy white blossoms were so light, pure and delicate. I realised how good is one of the country names of this umbelliferous plant, Queen Anne's Lace. The flower arrangement for the other wedding, in St. George's, Hanover Square, was a single vase of white marguerites, rather like the picture of Shasta daisies which I have described on page 66.

You will see opposite, a picture of a simple arrangement of foliage and seed heads. The central feature consists of the seed heads of the herb angelica, whose large tubular stems are cut and crystalised, and then they usually appear as cake ornaments. However, I grow it solely for its decorative qualities, for in addition to its valuable seed heads, it possesses fine bold foliage which in its second summer turns to primrose yellow.

The deeply cut leaves on either side of this group are those of two species of acanthus: *Acanthus mollis latifolius*, whose large lobed leaves are those which adorn the capitals of the columns in the Greek Corinthian style; and *Acanthus spinosus*, whose leaves, as the name suggests, are quite spiny. Spearing upwards are three leaves of the variegated water iris, *Iris pseudacorus variegatus*, which does not demand water round its roots, but grows happily in good damp garden soil. Lastly, to assist the upward movement of the iris leaves, I have used dried seed heads of one of our worst garden weeds—the common dock. When the dock seeds are still immature, I cut and dry them and find that they retain their vital colour.

◀ *Iris pseudacorus variegatus*

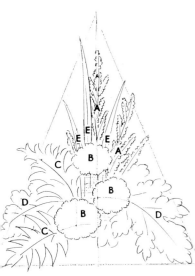

A. *Dried seed heads of dock*
B. *Dried seed heads of angelica*
C. *Leaves of Acanthus mollis latifolius*
D. *Leaves of Acanthus spinosus*
E. *Leaves of Iris pseudacorus variegatus*

Water lily

An Arrangement from the
Water Garden *Exquisite water lilies and bold leaves*

A water garden in August can be the most inspiring place for the keen flower arranger. The pond itself is just a larger version of our water-filled vessel. There is fine contrast in the foliage: submerged, in the case of the feathery water milfoil (myriophyllum); floating, as are the water lily leaves; or erect and dignified as the marginal reeds and irises. I particularly like the wonderful dark leaf of *Orontium aquaticum*, which has a luminous metallic sheen rather suggesting silvery fish fins on the upper surface, and an even paler under surface. If you can obtain this leaf it will certainly inspire you.

Though water lilies are such suitable flowers for arranging in vases they are quite unreliable, as one cannot depend upon them to stay open unless one takes certain steps. To make sure that they will not fail you at the crucial moment you may drop a small amount of paraffin wax (candle wax) at the base of each petal. This is a tricky and tedious operation but quite necessary unless you care to use the quicker method which I employed in the arrangement shown here. You will see that I gently everted the petals by thumb pressure, turning each concavity into a convexity. I must admit that it quite changes the character of the flower but will certainly save you much time and trouble.

When I was in Brisbane, Australia, I was given some wonderful tropical water lilies in shades of blue and pale pink, which I had great pleasure in arranging in a silver shell vase placed on a muslin cloth of pale blue. I had never before had such an opportunity and I wish I could show you a picture of it.

The leaves used here are those of the water plantain—*Alisma plantago-aquatica*, and the finer growth is provided by seed heads of the same plant. These may also be dried, but they need careful treatment as they are very brittle. Should you entangle two of these fragile things unravelling them will probably result in breakage of their stems. I have used these seed heads also for Christmas decoration, lightly painted with gum and sprinkled with glitter to give the effect of hoar frost.

If you can grow all these lovely pond plants you will have a wealth of material from which to select but do not overlook the lovely yellow and green striped iris, grown for the foliage rather than for the flower.

◀ *Alisma plantago-aquatica*

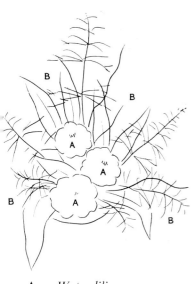

A.   *Water lilies*
B.   *Leaves and seed heads of*
       Alisma plantago-aquatica

Hydrangea macrophylla

Gay Decorations for Marquees

Brightly coloured flowers are massed together

Here are some ideas which might help you to decorate a marquee or village hall. The lower picture, as you can see, shows how you can make use of the pole which you will have in the marquee or tent. Two rings of crushed wire netting filled with damp moss, well soaked Florapak or Oasis form the basis for this decoration. The rings are hung by lengths of thick white cotton cord, which I obtained from my local draper. You may need more of these rings, but this depends of course on the size and height of the tent which you have to decorate. These rings take quite a large amount of plant material to furnish them suitably. A melange of dahlias, hydrangeas, golden yew and phlox were used here, passing the stems through the wire mesh to the soaked Florapak within. Treated thus, the flowers last for several days and need little attention. Now that we have Oasis, which is a green synthetic material, the problem of keeping flowers fresh, when it is difficult to place them in water, has been overcome to a large extent. Provided you soak Oasis really well for a few hours you can place it in a polythene bag and then stick your flower stems into it. It may be used hanging or in numerous other ways.

The top arrangement pictured has as a foundation a French imitation birdcage, in the base of which is a container filled with water and crushed wirenetting. This may also be used in decorating a church porch. You will naturally use such flowers as are in season at the time. I have used flowers of late summer; dahlias, hydrangeas, spiraea, and the double-flowered *Gypsophila* Bristol Fairy, a most delicate flower which has suffered much misuse. We have all seen gypsophila overcrowding a vase of sweet peas or roses to such an extent that we cannot see what is in the vase. You will see here a quite different and I think superior way to use it, in which the long sprays of lacey flowers neither confuse the pattern nor detract from the colour value of the flowers it accompanies.

Gypsophila is easily grown and makes a fine misty effect in the late summer flower border, where the double-flowered Bristol Fairy and the new pink flowered Flamingo both could find a place at a season when the garden is apt to begin looking a little tired after the great spate of flowers of late spring and early summer.

◀ *Gypsophila Bristol Fairy*

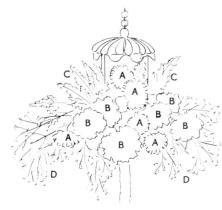

A. *Dahlias*
B. *Hydrangeas*
C. *Spiraea flowers*
D. *Gypsophila Bristol Fairy*

Assorted late summer flowers:
Dahlias, hydrangeas, phlox, and
foliage of the golden yew.

65

▲ *Chrysanthemum maximum Chiffon*

Shasta Daisies

Graceful grass flowers give a delicate effect

I can see that I have strayed somewhat from my original plan in writing this book. I had intended to give more emphasis to the individuality of each plant and the best way to bring out that character in one's arrangements. I do certainly get, in looking at a plant, the feeling that it must be used in one particular way. I think it is conditioned by my knowledge of the natural habit of the plant and how and where it grows. Nevertheless I am not a purist, and I do not think that one wild flower must necessarily always be accompanied by more wild flowers. I am here touching on the most difficult unrewarding subject of discussion—the question of taste; but my own instinctive feeling is to make as few restrictions as possible in the matter of choice of flowers.

In America the rules of flower arrangement are much stricter than is general in England. There they are forbidden to combine wild flowers, garden flowers, or hot house blooms in any one arrangement. Those who make such rules seem to have overlooked one thing: that somewhere in the world our most precious hot house subject is a wild plant such as mimosa or wattle in Australia and orchids in Ceylon. When I visited Ceylon, en route for Australia, I was asked to give a demonstration and talk in aid of the Y.W.C.A. I was confronted with masses of beautiful native orchids which I combined with some tropical fruits in an arrangement. The audience however were not impressed as they consider their orchids, even though wild plants, to be far too precious to be combined with mere fruits. So you just never know.

The daisy I have used is one which was a great favourite of my grandmother. She called it Phyllis Smith, but there is another similar one called Snow Princess which is obtainable from many nurseries which specialise in herbaceous plants. My grandmother used this flower to decorate a small Scottish church near her home. Daisies of any sort have what I call a 'face' and give interest and substance to an arrangement.

Daisies always look well with grasses, rather as if they were growing in the meadow. You will see that I have removed the rather coarse leaves from the Shasta daisy stems as this allows the flimsy, graceful grass flowers to have their full effect.

◀ *Chrysanthemum maximum Phyllis Smith*

Senecio leucostachys

Nerine Countess Maria Plater

Senecio laxifolius

Grey and Silver Foliage

Nerine lilies and rosy-pink sedum

Grey foliage plants are a great boon, and as many of them are 'evergreys' (one can hardly call them evergreen) they may contribute their decorative leaves even in the winter. I am constantly adding to the collection of grey-leaved plants in my garden, and I find the foliage most useful in arrangements which have flowers of either red, white, yellow, apricot, or pink colouring. It just is not possible to strike a discord with grey leaves, as it is only too easy to do with foliage of the more normal green hue.

Perhaps the easiest of grey-foliaged shrubs to grow in the garden is *Senecio laxifolius*, the foliage of which is elliptical, grey-green on the upper surface and white beneath even in the depths of winter. My collection also includes the large biennial Cotton Thistle, *Onopordon acanthium*, which takes up quite a lot of space with its large, prickly, metallic-looking leaves. For flower arrangement purposes the leaves of plants in their first year are more manageable, in their second year they are only suitable for the largest, most ambitious groups. This plant will seed itself about the garden but is not difficult

to eradicate where it is not wanted. Being very like a large Scottish thistle this plant was used in tubs to line the royal route to Holyrood Castle when the Queen visited Edinburgh after her Coronation.

The very pale foliage spraying out on either side of the base of this arrangement is that of *Senecio cineraria*. I always associate this plant with bedding schemes in seaside resorts and public parks, where it is often used with coleus, canna, croton or other plants with colourful foliage. *Senecio cineraria* is not really hardy, and it is well to take insurance cuttings to over-winter in a frame just in case the frost puts an end to the parent plant. *S. leucostachys* is very similar to *S. cineraria* and is equally good. The prominent lily-like flowers which you will see in the group are those of the pink flowered bulbous nerine, which is one of the most valuable garden bulbs ever to come from South Africa. At the heart of this group you will also find some pink roses and two heads of pink *Sedum spectabile*. The central top spike is of greenish-white mugwort, *Artemisia lactiflora*.

68

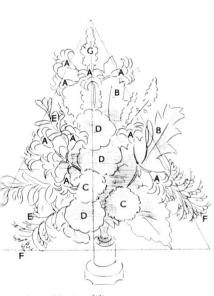

A. *Nerine lilies*
B. *Onopordon acanthium*
C. *Sedum spectabile*
D. *Rose*
E. *Senecio laxifolius*
F. *Senecio cineraria*
G. *Artemisia lactiflora*

▲ *Pompon dahlias*

◀ *Dahlia Dorothy Morris*

Richly-Coloured Dahlias

A harmony of brilliant hues

The garden varieties of the dahlia present every possible variation on the basic composite 'daisy' shape, and the range of colour is probably at least equal to that of any other cultivated plant. From one plant during the season one can cut so many long-stemmed blooms that they are most valuable in the flower arranger's garden. I find the many shades and tints of apricot which this plant provides are just what is needed to blend with the autumn leaves, seed heads and berries. Dahlias that I find particularly interesting are: Salmon Glory, a large cactus; Newby, a golden-apricot medium decorative; Jan Teulings, a chamois coloured small decorative; Arabian Night, blackish-crimson; Polar Beauty, a good white, as also are Virgo and Brumas. In this list I have not included any of the large decoratives, for though they are good flowers for flower show purposes, they are out of scale with most domestic settings, needing a setting more like the Albert Hall to do them justice.

In the top arrangement I have used three dahlias of the most intensely deep red variety Arabian Night, accompanied by four branches of *Pyracantha rogersiana*, close set with clusters of pale yellow berries; some peony foliage in its autumn colouring and several sprays of *Berberis thunbergii* richly flushed with autumnal red. The antique copper tea-pot is used to give height, as well as adding its lustrous colour.

In the lower arrangement I aimed at using a fiery harmony. This is easily achieved with dahlias as they provide a wonderful range of hot hues from which you may select fuel for your floral conflagration. The leaves are those of the kale that is used for cattle feed.

When I was in Australia recently I was surprised at the popularity of the dahlia. Even in the subtropical summer climate of Brisbane with a great wealth of showy plants to draw upon they favour the dahlia, which seems to be grown in every garden. In the flower market at Sydney I found that the stems of these flowers had all been given treatment with boiling water to enable the flowers to draw up the water without which they would have quickly flagged in that heat.

◀ *Cactus dahlias*

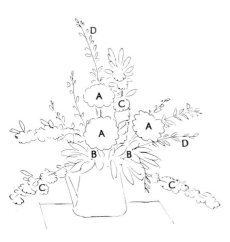

A. *Dahlia Arabian Night*
B. *Peony foliage*
C. *Pyracantha rogersiana*
D. *Berberis thumbergii*

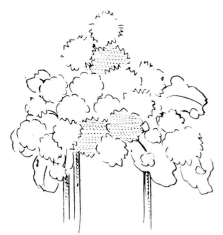

Assortment of dahlias in fiery hues, with leaves of kale

71

An October-flowering outdoor chrysanthemum

A November Group

Golden-orange chrysanthemums and russet leaves

The leaves in this November group opposite are of the horse chestnut. These handsome palmate leaves behave very well when pressed and sprays of beech leaves are also a favourite subject for this treatment. The leaves are placed between sheets of newspaper and then placed under the carpet in a place where they will be frequently trodden underfoot. Try to keep the leaves quite flat but if necessary it is possible to iron them out with a cool flat iron. Bracken is also responsive to this process, and you may pick the fronds at various stages of their development and so obtain a range of russet brown colours. I find that however well you press them they tend to curl when used in a very hot room and it is as well to have a good reserve supply for replacement purposes. Ferns other than bracken can be used and all press and dry excellently.

Another method of plant preservation is the glycerine and water process which gives very good results when used to treat beech or sweet chestnut. The treatment consists in hammering the woody stems and then placing them in a mixture of equal parts of glycerine and hot water. The evergreen cherry laurel responds to this treatment, but like the deciduous subjects mentioned it turns to a brownish colour. Branches with feathery seeds of our native *Clematis vitalba*, called Old Man's Beard, can be given this treatment but it is necessary to cut it before the fluffy winged seeds are ripe. I am told however that spraying with a laquer hair spray will make them secure should you have picked them rather late in their development. I am myself still experimenting with new subjects for this treatment, and I am not always completely successful. I have recently been given a very good tip. When you drain your car radiator of anti-freeze, save it and use it for preserving your beech leaves as it is excellent for this purpose.

Occasionally I see very good results obtained by others with rose hips and other berries in which the brilliant colour is retained.

To return to the picture. You will notice three incurved chrysanthemums, and some dried seed heads of the molucella arranged in an antique tea-caddy, in addition to the pressed horse chestnut leaves.

A. Incurved chrysanthemums
B. Pressed Horse Chestnut
    leaves
C. Dried Molucella laevis

73

▲ *Korean and Pompon chrysanthemums*

A Basket of Chrysanthemums

Natural sprays arrange themselves

The chrysanthemum has become an all the year round flower, and I must say I regret it. I should never buy these flowers which seem to epitomise autumn while there was all the wealth of flowers of spring and summer to be obtained. I actually find this reminder of autumn in June and July most depressing and I imagine many others must feel this too. However, there are obviously people of different mind numerous enough to make this out-of-season production of chrysanthemums profitable to the commercial growers.

The growing of the more normal autumn chrysanthemums both in the open and later under glass seems to be attracting more men of every income group each year. I say 'men' advisedly, for here surely is the man's flower par excellence and you may have heard them using the mysterious jargon terms which belong to the cultivation of chrysanthemums such as 'taking', 'stopping' etc. (I am told that 'taking' a bud actually means leaving it).

When it comes to arranging these flowers, the chrysanthemum has many virtues. There is first a good solid head of strong colour, fit to dominate any arrangement. Frequently there is a graceful pliant stem (sometimes, alas! a 'broomstick'). But above all their other virtues is their wonderful length of life as cut flowers. I use the chrysanthemum in its bronze and rich golden colours combined with the brown and russet of autumn foliage; with seeds heads and berries, bracken and beech leaves as shown elsewhere in this book.

Here is an arrangement of the small spraying type of chrysanthemum which is so popular in the United States. The same effect could have been produced if I had used the more common early-flowering kinds picked in the garden. I have arranged the flowers in a small basket which has, of course, an inner tin lining that holds enough water to keep them fresh. The open lid of this basket also helps to form an interesting textured background to this simple little group.

Among the outdoor varieties of chrysanthemum which I like best are the koreans and the rubellums. These are available in both single- and double-flowered forms with a range of colour including orange, copper, bronze, pink and white.

A basket of early-flowering chrysanthemums

▲ *Mixed hydrangeas*

Dried Flowers and Seed Heads

Hydrangeas form the focal point

Here is a large arrangement of assorted dried seed material built round a solid massing of hydrangea flower heads. You will also note the rounded artichoke flower head. I think these are so handsome that I take very special care in preparing them. The method is to cut the heads soon after they are open, for then the purple colour will be secured. Of course if you prefer brown colouring you may leave them somewhat longer on the plant. Dry these precious things separately suspending each by a string above the kitchen boiler to secure the quick desiccation which gives the best results. If however you pick them too late and then dry them too slowly you will be in trouble with the fluffy fruits, which will be released in large numbers on parachutes.

At the top of this group you will see the dried flowers of the acanthus or bear's breeches, which may be prepared by drying while the stems are in shallow water. Treated thus the whiteness of the blossoms is retained, though the rest of the plant becomes sear and brown. The grey-green colour of the artemisias; lamb's ears or *Stachys lanata;* and the eryngiums or sea hollies can be retained by careful treatment, and these look very well as an accompaniment to pink chrysanthemums.

With plantain lilies or hostas my method is to pick the seed heads before they open, and scatter their hosts of chaffy seeds. I then place them in a vessel with a little water to open out in the warmth of the kitchen. They look particularly delicate and lily-like as the capsules open widely and turn back to display the black winged seeds. The seed heads of the tulip may be treated in the same way, and, of course, there is no reason why you should not, if you have a garden and some patience, grow plants from the seeds which spill from the drying capsules.

The drying of flower heads is more difficult. The method which I find effective with achilleas is to place the stems in shallow water and sprinkle the flowers with a little powdered borax, which ensures that they retain their colour. This method of standing the very base of the stems in shallow water is also the only way I find infallible when dealing with the preparation of hydrangea flowers for winter use.

◀ *Clematis vitalba*

76

A. *Dried hydrangea flowers*
B. *Dried artichoke flower*
C. *Dried acanthus flowers*
D. *Eucalyptus leaves*
E. *Branch of Clematis vitalba*

Aspidistra lurida variegata

A Tropical Arrangement

Exotic anthuriums and house plants with alder catkins

The starting point of this modern flower arrangement was the gift of the three brilliant anthuriums. Because of their hard, definite form, glossy surface and rich scarlet colour I felt they needed the support of foliage equally firm, glossy and solid looking.

The anthurium is a dramatic plant and these gaudily bright spathes have most wonderful lasting qualities and show no change whatsoever after several weeks in use as cut flowers. Though they are much more at home in the stove house, the anthurium is one of the plants now pressed into service by those who supply room plants. As yet they are still rarities on an English windowsill, but they are not at all uncommon on Dutch ones. The anthurium's own dark green, handsome leaf is seen, here defining the lower angle upon the right of this triangular arrangement whose apex is formed by one of the pointed scarlet spathes.

How strange it is that the aspidistra and lace curtain, at one time stigmatised as middle class Victorian symbols of respectability, have both come back into favour. You will see that there are two of these wonderful variegated aspidistra leaves whose white stripes stand out so cleanly upon the green, smooth surface of the graceful foliage.

The central pale leafage is that of a coleus or hemp nettle, and in colour it is a beautiful lime green. Below the coleus is a large single *Begonia rex* leaf of the variety which is very fittingly called Iron Cross. The cross on the begonia leaf is almost black, and the rugose texture of this asymmetrical leaf is in complete contrast to all the smooth and polished surfaces of the other leaves used. Feeling that some lighter material would enhance the group I added some branches of alder catkins.

Having used so much material cut from stove house and room plants I will add a note on this very fashionable sort of gardening. The plants come from such different habitats and climates that some knowledge of their origin will probably give a guide to the best way to treat them in the highly artificial environment in which you are expecting them to grow and flourish. One worthwhile tip is to set your pot plants upon a bed of damp pebbles which will provide a microclimate in an otherwise dry environment. During the summer months, overhead spraying of the leaves is essential.

◀ *Anthurium andreanum*

A. *Spathes of anthurium*
B. *Anthurium leaf*
C. *Aspidistra leaf*
D. *Leaf of Begonia rex*
E. *Coleus plant*
F. *Philodendron laciniatum*
G. *Alder catkins*

Hedera helix sagittacfolia

An Indoor Garden

Different shapes and colours give lasting interest

Flat-dwellers deprived of the opportunity for natural outdoor gardening have probably been very largely responsible for the recent fashion in the house-plant cultivation. It is also true even of those who have gardens that when our garden plants are undergoing the rigours of the English winter the indoor plants give us the pleasure of seeing and smelling beautiful, fragrant living flowers at nose or eye level.

Here you will see the way in which I like to use my collection of room-plants, rather as though I had a planted miniature garden. In my jardinière filled with a good potting mixture I insert each of my chosen plants, knocking them out of their pots, not merely sinking the pot in the soil as many people do. I think it is very important to plant firmly. Thereafter careful watering is almost the only treatment needed. The watering of house plants is quite an art, for the roots must on no account be drowned and thus deprived of air but equally they must not be desiccated. Roughly, one can say water regularly in spring and summer with an overhead spray at least once a week; but from September to April plants will need much less water to keep them happy and healthy. It is important to keep all leaves dust-free, as quite a thin layer of dirt will deprive the plants of the already reduced sun-light under these conditions which is essential for their well-being. It is sometimes said that the breathing pores or stomata will be choked with the falling dust, but this does not happen to any extent since these pores are almost invariably on the underside of the leaf.

The lovely Indian azaleas are comparatively easy to water and fare best if the whole pot is occasionally submerged for ten minutes. You can tap the pot with a mallet to see if it gives a ringing note signifying that it needs water, but most people can tell by touching the soil surface with the fingers. Hydrangeas need even more frequent watering. I find it is a good thing with these plants to cover the blooms with sheets of damp paper. Hydrangeas love having their heads watered.

To return to our jardinière. The rockery effect is got by the use of pieces of bark and moss, and the occasional stone. The plants include maranta, sedum, zebrina, and various ivy plants.

◀ *Maranta leuconeura kerchoveana*

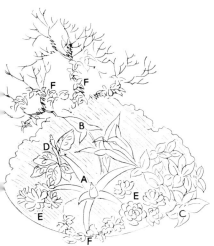

A. *Aechmea fulgens*
B. *Nephthytis*
C. *Zebrina pendula*
D. *Maranta leuconeura
      kerchoveana*
E. *Echeveria*
F. *Hedera helix sagittacfolia*

▲ *Aruncus sylvester* (*Spiraea aruncus*)

Dried Leaves and Seed Heads

Golden browns, silvers and pale golds

I constantly use dried materials in my arrangements, so I have made quite a serious study of methods of preserving plants, and also which plants are worthy of preserving.

As you may know seed heads usually behave well when dried, and are much easier to deal with than flower heads, though some of these are also good. In dealing with seed heads it is as well to let them get ripe before picking. After they are gathered they must be suspended upside down in a warm, well-aired room. Good colour in the final stage depends largely on drying the stuff as quickly as possible. It is most important to remove all foliage before drying for should you attempt this operation when the stems are dry and brittle you will crack and damage them.

All the following will, when dried, provide with their seed heads a range of muted browns and golden colours: delphiniums, sedums, hollyhocks, foxgloves, lupins, spiraeas, grasses, golden rods, aquilegias, irises, and the small bell-like seed heads of Spanish bluebells. From the hedgerows you may gather for drying seed heads of: docks, plantains, old man's beard, hemlock and cow parsley. I grow some annuals for drying such as atriplex, which has good red leaves in the summer garden and quite interesting seed heads which dry well. Bells of Ireland, *Molucella laevis*, I find rather more difficult than the general run of annuals to grow, but its beautiful parchment colour is well worth the care needed in picking off all leafage, and placing the stems in warm water to dry off—a procedure which seems contradictory but which I can recommend from experience. I find the hot atmosphere of a kitchen an ideal place for the drying operation.

From the vegetable garden some useful plants may be taken. Seed heads of brussels sprouts take a pale gold colour, and carrot, parsnip, leek, parsley, spinach, artichoke (globe) and angelica will all provide beauty in their dehydrated state.

In the group opposite you will find many of these seed heads, and in addition dried leaves of horse chestnut and beech, some silvery honesty pods, and a bracken frond, all forming a quiet harmony of colour to set against the complexity of patterned form which centres upon the dry golden-brown seed heads of *Achillea filipendulina*

◀ *Gathering angelica seed heads*

82

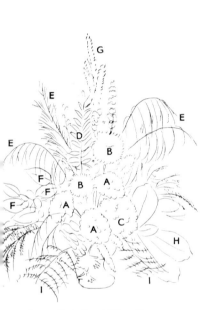

A. *Dried achillea flowers*
B. *Dried artichoke flowers*
C. *Dried angelica seed head*
D. *Dried lupin seed head*
E. *Dried grasses*
F. *Pressed beech leaves*
G. *Dried dock seed heads*
H. *Pressed horse chestnut leaves*
I. *Dried bracken*

Gentiana sino-ornata

Flowers with Short Stems

An early autumn collection

This little vase I filled in early autumn with bits and pieces from my garden. It is very pleasant to have a posy of this sort to cheer one, especially as one realises that there will not be many more such pickings before the months of winter scarcity are upon us. The double-flowered heather seen here is a variety of *Calluna vulgaris* called H. E. Beale which has a profusion of lovely fluffy (not bell-like) blossoms from August till October, and will, unlike most heathers, grow on a clay soil. I find it will dry quite well in the warmth of an average room, keeping its colour well, especially if placed in shallow water. It seems paradoxical to dry a plant for winter use while the base of its stems are in contact with water, but from experience I find this is quite a good way with many everlasting flowers and seed heads.

I have used some of the blossoms of the so-called autumn crocus, *Colchicum autumnale*, a rare native plant, which I have found on the hills in Gloucestershire. There are a number of foreign species and several hybrids with a wonderful tessellated pattern on their mauve pink flowers. I grow them in the grass as they are in nature meadow flowers, but they need careful placing as their large leaves which appear in spring must not be cut till they start to shrivel. They endure some shade, and may be planted among the shrubs, but not beneath the dense shade of large trees. The colouring is generally rose-lilac but they may be white, and are obtainable also in a double-flowered form. The flowers gain in effect by appearing well before the leaves, and Naked Ladies is one of the common names of the colchicum.

You will have noticed the six gentian flowers. These are *Gentiana sino-ornata*, which I grow where their lovely blue flowers can have some autumn sunshine. They send out lots of runners and from these you could easily increase your stock, and enjoy a mass planting of these valuable autumn flowers. *Gentiana acaulis*, is another lovely gentian and well worth while growing. Reginald Farrar says of it: 'If it grows fond of you it will flow over the garden like a wave of sky; if it does not like you it won't die, but it will live sulkily, grudgingly, peevishly, until you long to pick it up and throw it away'.

◀ *Calluna vulgaris H. E. Beale*

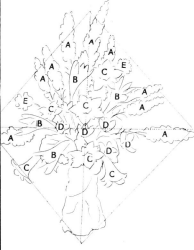

A.	*Calluna vulgaris H. E. Beale*
B.	*Autumn crocus*
C.	*Gentiana sino-ornata*
D.	*Cyclamen neapolitanum*
E.	*Viburnum fragrans*

85

▲ *Lilium auratum pictum*

▼ *Lilium auratum*

Lichen Twigs and Auratum Lilies

An arrangement in the Japanese style

Here is an extremely, almost starkly, simple arrangement which makes a welcome change from the more luxuriant flower groups employing foliage of various forms. It is not strictly Japanese, but owes something to the severe studious art of those gifted people. Stella Coe is a great artist and an expert in this style who has helped me to understand some of the principles of the art of Ikebana as the Japanese call it. I feel that this refined style is not suited to a relatively cluttered western interior and needs a plain spacious background to do it justice. There is very much more to Ikebana than just putting in twigs and a bloom; but we have not the background of flower symbolism which makes this art so much more to a Japanese than it can ever mean to us. I recently watched Sofu Teshigahara prune and trim one spray, and I was quite enthralled by the skill of this master, and felt that I could have profitably watched him for hours, and though it is a highly artificial style it achieves a strange effect of natural growth.

In this bleak design you will see that I have used four lichen-covered branches. I always make a point of collecting branches of good form covered with lichen where ever I can find them, and these four branches travelled back home in the car with me at the end of a holiday in Scotland. You will find that you can utilise such branches repeatedly in your arrangements as they last indefinitely. With the branches to give colour as well as contrast of form, you may arrange tulips, roses, dahlias, chrysanthemums, or such other flowers that happen to be in season. In my group I have used four of the lovely scented blooms of *Lilium auratum*, which I grew in my garden.

The branches and lilies are actually supported by some crushed, 2-inch mesh wire netting and a pin-holder within a water-filled jam dish, which in turn is placed on a flat pewter plate.

You will find it easy to arrange your branches and flowers at the required angles with the aid of the wire netting, and then cover this with a little moss. You may also care to add a piece of bracket fungus which is a parasite on birch trees and is called the birch tree polypore. Gather this bracket fungus dry or dry it off in a cool oven.

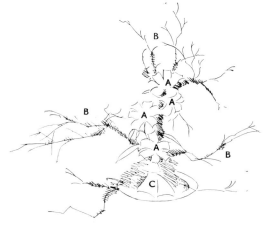

A. *Lilium auratum*
B. *Lichen-covered branches*
C. *Birch tree polypore*

▲ *Billbergia windii*

Contrasts in Texture

An unusual flower arrangement

This type of arrangement is not for everyone nor for every day of the week. It may most appropriately be used either in spring or, even more suitably, in autumn when rich colour is abundant. In fact, of course, we have all seen this kind of thing in church at the harvest festival service.

I have, however, sometimes used this unusual form of arrangement for a rather special luncheon party, when the tables were plain, solid, ancient oak refectory tables, and the background was the grey-green of tapestry-covered walls; a challenging but inspiring setting to test any flower arranger. I must admit that at first the guests were surprised to see an arrangement with only a few flowers, but it was not long before they recovered from the shock of strangeness, and many of them were generous in their admiration.

When we were decorating outdoor tables for barbecue meals in Australia we used this style of arrangement. It really looks most suitable and, unlike flowers, does not fade and wilt, nor is it easily blown over by the wind to spill water into the laps of unfortunate guests. There is, of course, just the slight risk that some less artistic member of the party may mistake it for a dessert course.

In the arrangement shown here there are russet brown skinned onions, whose smooth silkiness is contrasted to the roughness of the coconut; upturned mushrooms are there to reveal the dark brown radiating pattern of their gills; cauliflower provides another interesting piece of pattern, seeming like some greenish-ivory coloured coral. You will also find: grapes, apples, rhubarb and the nearly black fruits of the ivy in this group. For the flowers I chose rather exotic and strange billbergia blossoms in dark blue and lime green cascading out of their pink sheaths; and finally some apricot-coloured azalea flowers, two leaves of the purple canna, and a *Begonia rex* leaf. The group is set upon and around an inverted copper pan, whose burnished surface is lively with reflections.

I live in an old cottage and find there that this kind of decoration looks good and fitting, though I do feel that it is better not to use this somewhat special style too frequently.

◀ *Begonia rex*

88

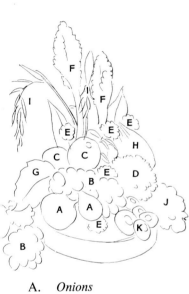

A. Onions
B. Grapes
C. Apples
D. Cauliflower
E. Ivy fruits
F. Rhubarb
G. Begonia rex leaf
H. Coconut
I. Billbergia
J. Azalea flowers
K. Mushrooms
L. Lemon

▲ *Carnations*

Carnations Have Prestige Value

Carnations, ivy fruits and alder catkins

I have given some consideration to the problem of arranging carnations because I am constantly being asked about effective ways of using them by people who find them stiff and unresponsive. I find also that many people are in much the same difficulty when they have to use daffodils. In both cases it is interesting to note that the natural foliage, though beautiful in itself, is often difficult to come by so a substitute has to be found. On the other hand from the point of view of the town dweller, or of those living in flats, these carnations are most useful as they are always obtainable. The carnation is, of course, the favourite buttonhole flower, and is frequently used in a bride's bouquet.

I was very amused recently to witness what respect was accorded to this flower. I had to spend a few weeks in hospital and while there kind friends gave me flowers. There were bunches of all kinds of sweet things such as lily-of-the-valley, gentians, etc, but what greatly impressed my fellow invalids that I really was one of the 'Top People' was when I was presented with a bunch of one dozen carnations. They have apparently enormous prestige value, and though I cannot pretend they are my favourite flower they have two great advantages: they are long-lasting and have sweet perfume.

Two things I have discovered about their use in arrangements: that they are so very much better with some unrelated foliage, and that they will not easily combine with any other flower. I have often been told that in certain flower combinations one flower will actually cause another to wilt and fade. I really cannot say that in my experience this is true. Or if it has happened I have perhaps put it down to death from natural causes. I have heard this particular accusation made against the wallflower, but I have personally only one objection to this plant as a cut flower and that is its woody stem which causes it to be very short lived in a vase. Knowing this weakness, however, I cut them very short and mass them in a box or basket.

In the arrangement shown I used as a foil to the flowers some sooty-black branches and cones of the water-loving alder, and a few nearly black, ripe fruits of the ivy.

◀ *Ivy fruits*

90

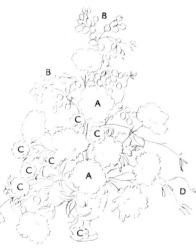

A. *Carnations*
B. *Dried alder catkins, female*
C. *Ivy fruits*
D. *Male alder catkins*

▲ *Carnation Peppermint Sim*

Carnations and Eucalyptus

Round, smooth leaves with frilly carnations

In this vase I have again used the same ten carnation flowers that appear in the arrangement on page 91, but this arrangement has some leaves of eucalyptus in place of the alder. I love any grey foliage but I used eucalyptus here because it is possible for anyone to buy it, but artemisia or grey onorpordon foliage would look just as well.

The colouring of the flowers—pale pink to white, freaked with flecking and pencilling is well contrasted to the silvery-green of the rounded disc-like leaves. The texture also is of interest with the flat smooth quietness of the leaves opposed to the frilly, almost fussy, flowers. The natural foliage or 'grass' of the carnation has almost the same hue as the eucalyptus leaves, but in shape it would be difficult to imagine any two forms more unlike. The leaves are those of *Eucalyptus polyanthemos*, which is grown in France largely for export to this country. It is the native blue gum tree of Australia. In the florist's shop it is generally obtainable from November to March, a time when it is most welcome.

The eucalyptus of Australia number over three hundred species, and a knowledge of them constitutes a special study. They grow so well in California that they are in danger of altering the landscape; for the blue gum is probably the quickest growing timber tree in the world in a climate which is to its liking, and there it will eventually reach a height of three hundred feet. Here in England the blue gum is not quite reliable, but it is well worth growing from seed, just to have its fine juvenile foliage for a year or so. The hardiest species is *Eucalyptus gunnii*, of which there is a flourishing specimen in Kew Gardens, though I always think that compared to the full luxuriance of the foliage of our native deciduous trees the leafage of the eucalyptus looks rather thin and inadequate.

I remember well an occasion when someone said to Mrs Spry, 'I understand that you don't like carnations'. Being a lover of all flowers Mrs Spry took this as a challenge. We arranged carnations for days with every imaginable background, and it was then that I realised how many ways there are of using this flower. Gone is the idea that the only fitting accompaniment for them is asparagus fern or smilax.

◀ *Carnation Jezabel*

A. Carnations
B. Eucalyptus leaves

93

Cypripedium Becky Clarke

A Touch of the Orient

Cypripedium in a bamboo container

This simple design is in an oriental style, and though the bamboo vase looks so completely Japanese it was, in fact, cut for me from the living plant in Australia where this type of container is very popular for flower arrangements. The branches bearing ripe larch cones can be made to take up almost any desired graceful line, unneeded branches being easily removed with the aid of secateurs. I have used two blooms of some rather special hybrid cypripedium orchids each with a wonderful pattern in deep red on its creamy petals. The canna leaves are also deep red in colour, while the single *Begonia rex* leaf is blotched with silver on a plum-coloured ground. I always grow a few of these *Begonia rex* plants in my kitchen. I cannot say that they really flourish; however, they do survive and this enables me to pick an occasional specimen of their unusual leaves.

Orchids are being used much more in flower groups than they were in the past, when we seldom saw them except in a lady's corsage spray. Their cultivation at one time was confined to those of wealth, but has now spread to more modest folk.

When I was in Ceylon I had the opportunity of using in a flower arrangement some wonderful sprays of a soft purple orchid with butterfly-like blooms which in that lovely island is a wild flower.

A table arrangement which I made some time ago was built around some yellow cypripedium orchids and mimosa flowers stripped of their leaves. This was placed on a mirror-glass table on which there was also a little group of lime green Venetian figures of minstrels. Our present Queen carried white orchids on her wedding day, and I have been told that one of the blooms was taken to America where it was most carefully preserved with the aid of borax. Later when the flower was exhibited at a New York orchid show the police had to be called to control the huge crowds that came to see it. It is an interesting fact that you can preserve flowers in this way. Shake some borax into a box just large enough for the flower; place your flower on this and submerge it gradually by sifting upon it more layers of borax. This method does not work with thick-petalled flowers. It is very similar to a method used by our ancestors who, however, used hot sand in place of borax.

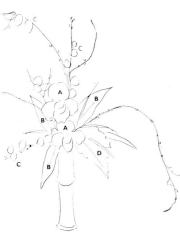

A. *Cypripedium orchids*
B. *Canna leaves*
C. *Larch*
D. *Begonia rex leaf*

▲ *White poinsettias*

White Poinsettias and Foliage

A green and white design

Centreing round the magnificent white poinsettias I have constructed a group of foliage, native and exotic and some lichen-covered branches. The actual flowers of the poinsettia are quite insignificant but just below them are the remarkable bracts which look so impressive in their usual intense red colouring, and no less so in the much more uncommon white form.

A few winters ago I did the flowers for a wedding of a special friend. Feeling worried as to what I could use I went to Thomas Rochford's nurseries and found I could have some of his then new poinsettias, which solved my problem. Mr Rochford introduced this new range of poinsettia colours from America—dusky pink, cream and white—and started growing them here. He now has large quantities available for the Christmas market. They add a wonderful focal point to the centre of any group and used with this collection of lovely hot house foliage plants they seem to be in keeping.

To ensure that my precious white poinsettias would live I did not cut them but merely washed the soil from the roots which I inserted bodily in the vase of water. Not only did they last for the wedding but for fully five weeks afterwards. Quite as important in the arrangement are the three leaves of the *Monstera deliciosa* a huge climber with aerial roots in its native South American jungle but now to be found in the English indoor garden. The monstera fruit is delicious to eat and the best specimens I have ever seen were standing well over 12 feet tall outside the town hall in Brisbane. Supporting leafage includes: *Magnolia grandiflora* leaves, *Elaeagnus pungens variegata*, perhaps the best evergreen variegated shrub we have; the perfoliate leaves of a eucalyptus; a spray of a variegated cordyline (or dracaena); and several sprays of the myrtle, associated with weddings since Roman times. For the wedding itself I had in addition several white arum lilies and sprays of forced white lilac, but these I have not included in this group; instead I have added my favourite lichen-covered branch.

◀ *Monstera deliciosa*

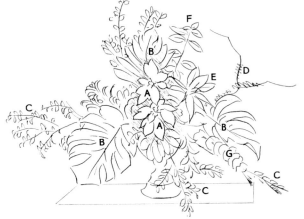

A. *White poinsettias*
B. *Monstera leaves*
C. *Myrtle leaves*
D. *Lichen-covered branch*
E. *Leaves of Magnolia grandiflora*
F. *Elaeagnus pungens variegata*
G. *Eucalyptus leaves*

▲ *Anemone coronaria*

An Outsize Posy

Variegated holly, chincherinchees and anemones

As you will see this posy is simply an outsize Christmas posy, complete with silvered paper posy frill and bows of scarlet satin ribbon with swallow tail ends. To make the lacy silver frill I cut out a disc of thin cardboard and on this I stuck several silver doyleys which I had cut to fit. I perforated the doyley disc to allow the flowers to be inserted, and then placed this over a small soup bowl of water in which was some crushed wire netting to give support to the plants.

The plants used are: anemones, from the florist; chincherinchees, also from the florist, and some variegated holly picked from a plant in my garden.

The chincherinchee is really a South African relation of our Star of Bethlehem, and its correct name is *Ornithogalum thyrsoides*. Its very strange common name of Chincherinchee is said to be an attempt to imitate the sound of the rustling plants when the wind blows across the veldt. The bulbs can be obtained for planting but as they flower in July there is such a wide choice of garden flowers then that the chincherinchee has nothing like the importance which it has when imported from South Africa arriving just at Christmas time.

I have wondered if one could treat them like roses, dipping the ends of the stems in melted paraffin wax (candle wax). If this were done just as the buds were bursting, and then they were placed in a box with the lid on in a cool place I have the feeling that they could be retarded successfully.

There are many varieties of variegated holly and I love them all. In fact a holly was the first tree I planted when I came to live in my cottage. One very good variegated holly is Waterer's Golden Weeping or *Ilex aquifolium aurea pendula* which has a fine graceful arching habit; another is Perry's Weeping Silver or *I. a. argentea pendula*. The Golden Hedgehog or *I. a. ferox aurea* is interesting as it has prickles on the leaf surface as well as on the margin, and Golden Queen, *I. a. aurea regina*, is very good. Do not be misled by the name queen into thinking the plant is a female and, therefore, berry-bearing. It is not always realised by gardeners that the holly bears either male, pollen-bearing flowers or female flowers which will produce berries.

◀ *Ornithogalum thyrsoides*

A. *Anemones*
B. *Chincherinchees*
C. *Holly*

Ilex argentea marginata

(Left) *The wire coat hanger before treatment.* (Centre) *The triangle has been converted into a circle. It is not necessary to take very great trouble to obtain a perfect circle as the leaves will cover the wire completely. This shows the wreath half bound with pendant pieces of evergreen.* (Right) *The door-knocker has been completed and a large ribbon bow attached to the wire at the place where the hook protrudes. When hung in place, the ribbon should be adjusted to obscure the hook.*

Christmas Decorations

Candles for the table and a wreath for the door

Here the containers are two glass bowls with stems. To secure the candles I pressed a large piece of plasticine into the centre of each bowl and the candles are inserted firmly into this. It is most essential to take great care when using lighted candles, especially if the guests include children excitedly pulling Christmas crackers.

Around the tall candles I have grouped a combination of variegated holly, sprays of red holly berries, chincherinchees and Christmas roses. Separate sprays of holly berries were added as the particular variegated holly shown here is a male form. To give an appropriate appearance of snowy sparkle I lightly applied gum to the leaves and sprinkled them with glass glitter. If you are not using variegated holly you may like to add some touches of white to the edges of the green leaves. I find shoe white most suitable as it has the great advantage, especially when children are helping, that it easily washes off. You can now obtain a Christmas 'snow' in the form of an aerosol spray. It is excellent, easy to use, but rather expensive.

The drawings show three stages in the conversion of a coat hanger into a door-knocker wreath. In parts of Germany and in the Scandinavian countries this welcoming door-knocker wreath has long been in use. The method of pressing into service those wire hangers, which by having clothes cleaned you cannot help but accumulate, comes from the United States of America.

First you fashion the triangle into a circle by manipulating the wire with your fingers. You next cut small pieces of various evergreens into four-inch sprays and bind them onto the circular foundation with fuse wire. You must start from the top and bind very tightly until you have completed a semicircle. Then repeat the process on the other side. Having clothed the wire frame decently in leafage, finish the wreath off with a good large bow of ribbon. Scarlet ribbon is very effective but to some extent the choice of colour must be related to the door against which it will be displayed. The hook is, of course, most useful but should not be prominent. It is easily concealed by the ribbon.

A. *Christmas roses*
B. *Chincherinchees*
C. *Variegated holly*

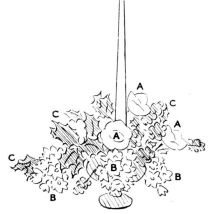

Index

The figures in parentheses indicate illustration pages

Acanthus flowers, dried, 76, (77)
  mollis latifolius, 60, (61)
  spinosus, 20, (20), (21), 60, (61)
Achillea, 20, (21), 36, (37), 56, (57)
  fiilipendulina, dried, 82
  flower heads, (83)
   preserving, 76
Aechmea fulgens, (81)
Alder catkins, 78, (79), 90, (91)
Alisma plantago-aquatica, 62, (62), (63)
Amaranthus caudatus, 58, (58)
  albiflorus, 58, (59)
Amaryllis, 40, (41)
Anemone blanda, 14, (15)
  scythinica, (14)
  coronaria, 98, (98), (99)
Angelica archangelica, 60, (60), (61)
  seed heads, 82, (82), (83)
Anthurium andreanum, 78, (78), (79)
Anti-freeze, for preserving, 72
Antirrhinum, 56, (57)
Apple blossom, 32, (33)
Apples, 88, (89)
Aquilegia, seed heads, preserving, 82
Artemisia, foliage, 92
  lactiflora, 68, (69)
  preserving, 76
Arum italicum, 22, (23)
  resting, 22
  lilies, 16, (16), (17)
   hardy, 16
Aruncus sylvester, (82)
Aspidistra lurida variegata, 78, (78), (79)
Atriplex, preserving, 82
Aucuba japonica variegata, 20, (20), (21)
Autumn crocus, 84, (85)
Azalea flowers, 88, (89)

Bamboo container, 94, (95)
Barberton daisies, 52, (53)
Bark, 24, (25)
Basket, 9
  arrangement, 56, (57), 74, (75)
Bear's Breeches, 20
  dried, 76, (77)
  preserving, 76
Beech leaves, dried, 82, (83)
  preserving, 72
Begonia rex, 78, (79), 88, (88), (89), 94, (95)
Berberis thunbergii, 70, (71)
Berries, preserving, 72
Billbergia, 88, (89)
  windii, (88)
Birch tree polypore, 86, (87)
Blue gum, 92
Bocconia, 36
Boiling water treatment, 42, 70
Borax, 76, 94
Bracken, 72, (83)
Bracket fungus, 86, (87)
Brussels sprouts, seed heads, preserving, 82

Cabbage, 12, (13)
Calluna vulgaris, preserving, 84
  H. E. Beale, 84, (84), (85)
Camellia japonica Elegans, (10)
  foliage, 10
  japonica Mathotiana alba, (10)
  Trail, The, 10
  williamsii Citation, (10)
Camellias, site for, 10
Candles, 100, (101)
Cannas, 94, (94), (95)
  leaves, 88, (89)
Cardoons, 20, (21)

Carnations, (27), 36, (37), 90, (90), (91), 92 (92), (93)
Carrots, seeds heads, preserving, 82
Catkins, *see* Alder, Hazel
Cauliflower, 88, (89)
Chaenomeles speciosa, (31)
Cherry laurel, 20, (21)
  preserving, 72
Chimonanthus fragrans, 22, (22), (23)
Chincherinchees, 98, (98), (99), 100, (101)
Christmas decorations, 100, (100), (101)
  roses, 22, 100, (101)
Chrysanthemum maximum Chiffon, (66)
  Phyllis Smith, 66, (66), (67)
Chrysanthemums, 72, (72), (73)
  early-flowering, 74, (74), (75)
  Korean, 74, (74)
  Pompon, (74)
Clematis, (43), 49
  vitalba, (76), (77)
  preserving, 72
Coat hanger, use of, 100, (100)
Coconut, 88, (89)
Colchicum autumnale, 84, (85)
Coleus, 78, (79)
Colour, arrangement of, 38
Containers, 9
  basket, 56, (57)
Convallaria majalis, 28, (28), (29)
Cordyline, 96, (97)
Cork, 24, (25)
Corylopsis glabrescens, 18, (18), (19)
Corylus avellana, (16)
Cotton Thistle, 68, (69)
Cow parsley, seed heads, preserving, 82
Crinum capense, 49
  Flowers (51)

Crocus tomasinianus, 14, (15)
Crown Imperials, 40, (40), (41)
Cyclamen neapolitanum, (85)
Cypripedium orchids, 94, (94), (95)

Daffodils, 24, (24), (25)
  in bowls, 24
Dahlias, 64, (65)
  boiling water treatment, 70
  Cactus, (70), (71)
  Pompon, (70), (71)
Dances, flowers for, 48
Daphne mezereum, 18
Delphiniums, 48, (50), 56, (56), (57)
  seed heads, dried, 82
Dianthus barbatus, 42, (42), (43)
Dock, seed heads, dried, (21), 60, (61), (83)
  preserving, 82
Dracaena, 96, (97)
Dried flowers, 20, (21), 76, (77)
  leaves, 20, (21)
  materials, 76, (77)
  seed heads, 76, (77)

Echeveria, (81)
Elaeagnus pungens variegata, 96, (97)
Elder flowers, (50)
Erica carnea, 30, (30), (31)
Eryngiums, preserving, 76
Eucalyptus, (13), 77, 96, (97)
  globulus, 12
  gunnii, 12, 92
  perriniana, 12, (12)
  polyanthemos, 92, (93)
  populifolia, 12
Evergreen, sponging leaves of, 20
Everlasting pea, 38, (38), (39)

Ferns, preserving, 72
Florapak, 9, 64
Focal point, 38
Foliage, arum, 40
  bergenia, 40
  cleansing, 20
  glossy, 10, (11)
  grey, 12, 68, (69), 76, 92, (93)
  mahonia, 18
Forsythia, 26, (26)
Foxgloves, 42, (43), 48, (48), (50)
  seed heads, preserving, 82
  sowing, 48

Freesias, 28, (29)
Fritillaria imperialis, 40, (40), (41)

Galanthus nivalis, (14)
  maximus, 14, (15)
Garrya elliptica, 12, (12), (13)
  site for, 12
Gentiana, 84, (84), (85)
Gerbera jamesonii, 52, (52), (53)
Gladiolus, 36, (36), (37)
Glass glitter, 100
Globe artichoke, dried, 76, (77), 82, (83)
Glycerine, for preserving, 72
Golden rod, preserving, 82
Gorse, (14), 40
Grape hyacinth, 14, 30, (31)
Grapes, 54, (55), 88, (89)
Grasses, 66, (67), (83)
  preserving, 82
Guelder rose, 26, (26), (27)
Gypsophila, 64, (64), (65)

Hamamelis mollis, 30, (30), (31)
Hazel catkins, 16, (16), (27)
Heather, 18, (19), 30
Hedera helix conglomerata, 52, (52), (53)
  sagittaefolia, 80, (80), (81)
Helleborus foetidus, 20, (21), 22, (31)
  culture of, 30
  niger, 22, (23)
  culture of, 22
  orientalis, 22, (22)
Hemlock, seed heads, preserving, 82
Hemp nettle, 78, (79)
Herbaceous plants, 56, (56), (57)
Hermodactylus tuberosus, 14, (15)
Hippophae rhamnoides, 52, (53)
Holly, 20
  variegated, 98, (99)
Hollyhocks, seed heads, preserving, 82
Honesty pods, dried, 82, (83)
Horse chestnut leaves, dried, 82, (83)
  pressed, 72, (73)
Hostas, seed heads, preserving, 76
House plants, 78, (78), (79), 80, (80), (81)
Hyacinth, 26, (27), 28, (29), (31)
Hydrangea, 20, (21), 49, (51), 56, (57), 58, (59)
  dried, (77)
  flower heads, preserving, 76
  macrophylla, 64, (64), (65)
  watering, 80

Ikebana, 86
Ilex, 98, 100, (100), (101)
Indian azaleas, watering, 80
Iris, bearded, 42, (43)
  histrio, 14
  histrioides, 14
  major, 14, (14)
  pseudacorus variegatus, 60, (60), (61)
  seed heads, preserving, 82
  striped, 62
  susiana, 34, (34), (35)
  culture of, 34
Italian arum, 22, (23)
Ivy fruits, (29), 88, (89), 90, (90), (91)

Japanese flower arrangement, 86
Jardinière, 80, (81)
Jasmine, 46, (46), (47), 56, (57)
Jasminum officinale, 46, (46), (47)

Kale, 12
  leaves, 70, (71)
Kenzan, 9

Lacquer hair spray, for preserving, 72
Lamb's Ears, preserving, 76
Larch, (95)
Lathyrus latifolius, 38, (38), (39)
Leaves, dried, 82, (83)
  pressing, 72
  skeletonised, (45)
  skeletonising, 44
Leeks, seed heads, preserving, 82
Lemon, (89)
Lenten Rose, 22
Lichen, 86, (87), 96, (97)
Lilac, 34, (34), (35)
Lilies, seed heads, preserving, 76
Lilium auratum, 16, 86, (86), (87)
  pictum, 86
  longiflorum, 49, (49), (51)
  regale, 16, 56, (56), (57)
Lily-of-the-Valley, 28, (28), (29)
  tree, 28
Lime flowers, 38, (39), 49, (50), (51)
Love-lies-Bleeding, 58, (58), (59)
Lupins, 42, (42), (43)
  seed heads, preserving, 82
Lysichitum camtschatcense, 40, (40), (41)

Macleaya cordata, 36, (36), (37)
Madonna Lily, 16
Magnolia grandiflora, leaves, 44, (45), 96, (97)
Mahonia japonica, 18, (18), (19)
Maranta leuconeura kerchoveana, 80, (80) (81)
Marquees, 64, (65)
Molucella laevis, 72, (72), (73), 82
Monstera deliciosa, 96, (96), (97)
Moss, 24, (25)
Mourning widow iris, 14
Muscari, 30, (31)
 azureum, 14, (15)
Mushrooms, 88, (89)
Myrtle, 96, (97)

Naked Ladies, 84, (85)
Narcissus, 14, (15), 26, (27), (31), *see* also Daffodils
Nephthytis, (81)
Nerine, 68, (68), (69)

Oasis, 9, 64
Old Man's Beard, preserving, 72, 82
Olive oil, use of, 20
Onions, (89)
Onopordon acanthium, 68, (69)
 foliage, 92
Orchids, preserving, 94
Ornithogalum thyrsoides, 98, (98), (99)
Orontium aquaticum, 62

Parsley, seed heads, preserving, 82
Parsnip, seed heads, preserving, 82
Party flowers, 48, 49, (50), (51)
Passiflora caerulea, 54, (54), (55)
Passion flower creeper, 54, (54), (55)
Peonies, 38, (38), (39), (50)
 foliage, 71, (71)
 treatment of, 49
Petasites fragrans, 30, (31)
Philadelphus, 48, (50)
 speciosus, (48)
Philodendron laciniatum, (79)

Phlox, 56, (57), (65)
 rosea superba, (56)
Phytolacca americana, 58, (59)
Picture frame, use of, 42, (43)
Pieris formosa forrestii, 28
 japonica, 18, (18), (19), 28, (29)
Pin-holder, 86
Plantain, seed heads, preserving, 82
Plasticine, 100
Plume Poppy, 36, (36), (37), 39
Poinsettias, 96, (96), (97)
Polyanthus, 30, (30), (31)
Poppies, 42, (43)
Posy, 98, (99)
Pussy Willow, 26, (26)
Pyracantha rogersiana, 70, (71)

Red Ink Plant, 58, (58), (59)
Regal Lily, 56, (56), (57)
Rhododendron, 18, (19)
Rhubarb, 88, (89)
Rose hips, preserving, 72
Roses, (35), 36, (36), (43), 44, (44), (45), 54, (55), 56, (57), (69)
 moss, 46
 old-fashioned, 46, (47)
 rambler, 49, (50)

Salix caprea, 26, (26)
Sea Buckthorn, 52, (53)
Sea Holly, preserving, 76
Sedum, 80, (81)
 maximum atropurpureum, 58, (58), (59)
 spectabile, 58, (58), (59), 68, (69)
Sedums, seed heads, dried, 82
Seed heads, dried, 76, (77), 82, (83)
Senecio cineraria, 68, (69)
 laxifolius, 68, (68), (69)
 leucostachys, 68, (68)
Shasta daisies, 66, (67)
Shell container, 52, (53)
Shingle, 16, 24
Shoe white, 100
Slugs, 22
Spinach, seed heads, preserving, 82
Spiraea, (65), (82)

Stachys lanata, preserving, 76
Stems, short, 84
Strawberry grape, 54, (55)
Sweet Chestnut, preserving, 72
Sweet Williams, 42, (42), (43)
Syringa prestoniae, 34

Thalictrum, 56, (57)
 speciosissimum, 36, (37)
Tiger Lily, 16
Transvaal daisy, 52, (53)
Tulips, 28, (28), (29), 32, (32), (33), (35)
 seed heads, preserving, 76

Vases, 9, *see* also Containers
 placing, 48
 wall, 49, (50)
Vegetables, decorative, 12
Veratrum nigrum, 20
Verbascum, 56, (57)
Veronica, (31)
Viburnum fragrans, 54, (54), (55), (85)
 opulus sterile, 26, (26), (27), (29)

Wallflowers, 90
Wall vase, 49, (50)
Waterhouse, Mr., 10
Water lilies, 62, (62), (63)
Weddings, flowers for, 48, 60
Wheat ears, 54, (55)
Wilting of flowers, 90
Winter heliotrope, 30, (31)
 Sweet, 22, (22), (23)
Wire netting, use of, 9
Witch Hazel, 30, (30), (31)
Wreath, Christmas, 100, (100)

Yew, golden, (65)
Yucca flaccida, 49, (49), (51)

Zantedeschia aethiopica, (16)
 elliottiana, 40, (41)
Zebrina pendula, (81)